U.S. POLICY TOWARD TIBET: ACCESS, RELIGIOUS FREEDOM, AND HUMAN RIGHTS

HEARING

BEFORE THE

SUBCOMMITTEE ON ASIA AND THE PACIFIC

OF THE

COMMITTEE ON FOREIGN AFFAIRS
HOUSE OF REPRESENTATIVES

ONE HUNDRED FIFTEENTH CONGRESS

FIRST SESSION

DECEMBER 6, 2017

Serial No. 115–102

Printed for the use of the Committee on Foreign Affairs

Available via the World Wide Web: http://www.foreignaffairs.house.gov/ or
http://www.gpo.gov/fdsys/

U.S. GOVERNMENT PUBLISHING OFFICE

27–756PDF   WASHINGTON : 2018

For sale by the Superintendent of Documents, U.S. Government Publishing Office
Internet: bookstore.gpo.gov   Phone: toll free (866) 512–1800; DC area (202) 512–1800
Fax: (202) 512–2104   Mail: Stop IDCC, Washington, DC 20402–0001

COMMITTEE ON FOREIGN AFFAIRS

EDWARD R. ROYCE, California, *Chairman*

CHRISTOPHER H. SMITH, New Jersey
ILEANA ROS-LEHTINEN, Florida
DANA ROHRABACHER, California
STEVE CHABOT, Ohio
JOE WILSON, South Carolina
MICHAEL T. McCAUL, Texas
TED POE, Texas
DARRELL E. ISSA, California
TOM MARINO, Pennsylvania
MO BROOKS, Alabama PAUL
COOK, California SCOTT
PERRY, Pennsylvania RON
DeSANTIS, Florida
MARK MEADOWS, North Carolina
TED S. YOHO, Florida
ADAM KINZINGER, Illinois
LEE M. ZELDIN, New York
DANIEL M. DONOVAN, JR., New York
F. JAMES SENSENBRENNER, JR.,
  Wisconsin
ANN WAGNER, Missouri
BRIAN J. MAST, Florida
FRANCIS ROONEY, Florida
BRIAN K. FITZPATRICK, Pennsylvania
THOMAS A. GARRETT, JR., Virginia
JOHN R. CURTIS, Utah

ELIOT L. ENGEL, New York
BRAD SHERMAN, California
GREGORY W. MEEKS, New York
ALBIO SIRES, New Jersey
GERALD E. CONNOLLY, Virginia
THEODORE E. DEUTCH, Florida
KAREN BASS, California
WILLIAM R. KEATING, Massachusetts
DAVID N. CICILLINE, Rhode Island
AMI BERA, California
LOIS FRANKEL, Florida
TULSI GABBARD, Hawaii
JOAQUIN CASTRO, Texas
ROBIN L. KELLY, Illinois
BRENDAN F. BOYLE, Pennsylvania
DINA TITUS, Nevada
NORMA J. TORRES, California
BRADLEY SCOTT SCHNEIDER, Illinois
THOMAS R. SUOZZI, New York
ADRIANO ESPAILLAT, New York
TED LIEU, California

AMY PORTER, *Chief of Staff*   THOMAS SHEEHY, *Staff Director*
JASON STEINBAUM, *Democratic Staff Director*

————

SUBCOMMITTEE ON ASIA AND THE PACIFIC

TED S. YOHO, Florida, *Chairman*

DANA ROHRABACHER, California
STEVE CHABOT, Ohio
TOM MARINO, Pennsylvania
MO BROOKS, Alabama
SCOTT PERRY, Pennsylvania
ADAM KINZINGER, Illinois
ANN WAGNER, Missouri

BRAD SHERMAN, California
AMI BERA, California
DINA TITUS, Nevada
GERALD E. CONNOLLY, Virginia
THEODORE E. DEUTCH, Florida
TULSI GABBARD, Hawaii

C O N T E N T S

Page

WITNESSES

Mr. Richard Gere, chair of the Board of Directors, International Campaign for Tibet 10
Mr. Tenzin Tethong, director of the Tibetan Service, Radio Free Asia 20
Mr. Carl Gershman, president, National Endowment for Democracy 25

LETTERS, STATEMENTS, ETC., SUBMITTED FOR THE HEARING

The Honorable Ted S. Yoho, a Representative in Congress from the State of Florida, and chairman, Subcommittee on Asia and the Pacific: Prepared statement 3
Mr. Richard Gere: Prepared statement 14
Mr. Tenzin Tethong: Prepared statement 22
Mr. Carl Gershman: Prepared statement 27

APPENDIX

Hearing notice 46
Hearing minutes 47
The Honorable Eliot L. Engel, a Representative in Congress from the State of New York: Prepared statement 48
The Honorable Gerald E. Connolly, a Representative in Congress from the Commonwealth of Virginia: Prepared statement 50
Questions for the record submitted by the Honorable Dina Titus, a Representative in Congress from the State of Nevada 52

U.S. POLICY TOWARD TIBET: ACCESS, RELIGIOUS FREEDOM, AND HUMAN RIGHTS

WEDNESDAY, DECEMBER 6, 2017

House of Representatives,
Subcommittee on Asia and the Pacific,
Committee on Foreign Affairs,
Washington, DC.

The subcommittee met, pursuant to notice, at 2:40 p.m., in room 2172, Rayburn House Office Building, Hon. Ted Yoho (chairman of the subcommittee) presiding.

Mr. YOHO. The subcommittee will come to order. Members present will be permitted to submit written statements to be included in the official hearing record.

Without objection, the hearing record will remain open for 5 calendar days to allow statements, questions, and extraneous material for the record, subject to length limitations in the rules.

As a friendly reminder, I would like to remind audience members that disruption of committee proceedings is against the law and will not be tolerated. Although wearing themed shirts while seated in the hearing room is permissible, holding up signs during the proceedings is not. Any disruptions will result in suspension of the proceedings until Capitol Police can restore order.

With that, I would like to say good afternoon and thank you to my colleagues and the panel for joining us here today for this discussion of Tibet. It is a turbulent time in international relations, particularly in the Asia-Pacific region where security concerns dominate policy discussions daily. In this environment, some important issues are getting far too little attention, especially on the international stage, and the status of Tibet is one of these issues. It is an important moment to shine a light on the events in Tibet, especially with significant legislation on this topic pending before this committee.

Tibet's exiled spiritual leader, the 14th Dalai Lama, and other Tibetan leaders in exile convened a first of its kind conference in October, the Five-Fifty Forum. The objective was to establish a 5-year plan for negotiations with China on Tibet's future or, if negotiations fail, a plan for 50 more years of resistance. The context of these discussions is a period of increased uncertainty about Tibet's future. The Dalai Lama has advocated a compromise, called the Middle Way, seeking autonomy within China for the people of Tibet rather than independence from China.

But the Tibetan people and the world are increasingly forced to consider what will happen after the Dalai Lama's leadership. It is still unknown how the Dalai Lama will choose to determine his succession and reincarnation, but China, having kidnapped the Panchen Lama as a child in 1995 and put an imposter in his place, may attempt to appoint a fraudulent successor. A result that is seen as illegitimate or intolerable by the people of Tibet could cause a wave of protest and resistance, ushering in new heights of oppression.

Human rights and personal freedoms in Tibet are already in a poor and worsening state. According to the State Department's 2016 Human Rights Report, the Government of China engages in the severe repression of Tibet's unique religious, cultural, and linguistic heritage by, among other means, strictly curtailing the civil rights of the Tibetan population, including the freedoms of speech, religion, association, assembly, and movement. The authorities have used heavy-handed and violent tactics to maintain control in Tibet, especially in response to unrest, including extrajudicial killings, torture, arbitrary arrests, extrajudicial detentions, and house arrests. And Tibet remains extremely isolated. The flow of information in and out of Tibet is tightly restricted. Tibetans are prevented from obtaining passports and moving freely, and foreigners, especially journalists and officials, are frequently denied access. I hope that today the panel can provide the subcommittee with suggestions for policy Congress can pursue to push back against these abuses that we see too often coming out of China.

Fortunately, there are two pieces of legislation pending before the subcommittee that aim to do just that, and I look forward to the witnesses and their impressions of these bills. Representative McGovern's Reciprocal Access to Tibet Act of 2017 would promote access to Tibetan areas by denying U.S. visas to Chinese Government officials who are involved in restricting access to Tibet. And Chairman Emeritus Ros-Lehtinen's H. Con. Resolution 89 provides comprehensive reassertion of U.S. policies toward Tibet, underscoring the importance of the Tibetan Policy Act and clarifying the sense of Congress on a number of important issues relating to Tibet.

In addition to these measures, I am looking forward to hearing suggestions for other actions the subcommittee may take to advance human rights, religious freedom, and access in Tibet. Once again, I would like to thank our panel for joining us today and for your patience while we had to go down and do our constitutional duty of voting.

And, without objection, the witnesses' written statements will be entered into the hearing record.

And I now turn to my ranking member and friend for any remarks he may have, Mr. Sherman.

[The prepared statement of Mr. Yoho follows:]

<u>**U.S. Policy Towards Tibet: Access, Religious Freedom, and Human Rights**</u>
Subcommittee on Asia and the Pacific
House Committee on Foreign Affairs
Wednesday, December 6, 2017, 2:00 p.m.
Opening Statement of Chairman Ted Yoho

Good afternoon and thank you to my colleagues and the panel for joining us today for this discussion of Tibet. It is a turbulent time in international relations, particularly in the Asia-Pacific region, where security concerns dominate policy discussions. In this environment, some important issues are getting far too little international attention. The status of Tibet is one of these issues.

It is an important moment to shine a light on events in Tibet, especially with significant legislation on this topic pending before the Committee. Tibet's exiled spiritual leader, the 14th Dalai Lama, and other Tibetan leaders in exile convened a first-of-its kind conference in October, the Five-Fifty Forum. The objective was to establish a five-year plan for negotiations with China on Tibet's future. Or, if negotiations fail, a plan for 50 more years of resistance.

The context of these discussions is a period of increased uncertainty about Tibet's future. The Dalai Lama has advocated a compromise approach called the "Middle Way," seeking autonomy within China for the people of Tibet, rather than independence from China. But the Tibetan people and the world are increasingly forced to consider what will happen after the Dalai Lama's leadership. It is still unknown how the Dalai Lama will choose to determine his succession and reincarnation.

But China, having kidnapped the Panchen Lama as a child in 1995 and put an imposter in his place, may attempt to appoint a fraudulent successor. A result that is seen as illegitimate or intolerable by the people of Tibet could cause a wave of protest and resistance, ushering in new heights of oppression.

Human rights and personal freedoms in Tibet are already in a poor, and worsening state. According to the State Department's 2016 human rights report, the government of China engages in "the severe repression of Tibet's unique religious, cultural, and linguistic heritage by, among other means, strictly curtailing the civil rights of the Tibetan population, including the freedoms of speech, religion, association, assembly, and movement."

The authorities have used heavy-handed and violent tactics to maintain control in Tibet, especially in response to unrest, including extrajudicial killings, torture, arbitrary arrests, extrajudicial detention, and house arrests. And Tibet remains extremely isolated. The flow of information in and out of Tibet is tightly restricted, Tibetans are prevented from obtaining passports and moving freely, and foreigners, especially journalists and officials, are frequently denied access.

I hope that today, the panel can provide the Subcommittee with suggestions for policies Congress can pursue to push back against these abuses. Fortunately, there are two pieces of legislation pending before the Subcommittee that aim to do just that, and I look forward to hearing the witnesses' impressions of these bills.

Representative McGovern's Reciprocal Access to Tibet Act of 2017 would promote access to Tibetan areas by denying U.S. visas to Chinese government officials who are involved in restricting access to Tibet. And Chairman-emeritus Ros-Lehtinen's H.Con.Res.89 provides a comprehensive reassertion of U.S. policy towards Tibet, underscoring the importance of the Tibetan Policy Act and clarifying the sense of Congress on a number of important issues relating to Tibet.

In addition to these measures, I'm looking forward to hearing suggestions for other actions the Subcommittee might take to advance human rights, religious freedom, and access in Tibet. Once again, I thank the panel for joining us today, and now turn to Ranking Member Sherman for his remarks.

Mr. SHERMAN. Thank you, Mr. Chairman, for holding these hearings on this important issue of American policy and human rights. Ten years ago, in October 2007, Congress awarded His Holiness the Dalai Lama the Congressional Gold Medal in recognition of his outstanding contributions to peace, nonviolence, human rights, and religious understanding.

Unfortunately, in the decade since, China's suppression of Tibet has continued and intensified. China has not held discussions about Tibet's status with the Dalai Lama's representatives since January 2010. In 2015, China stated that there is no prospect of granting much autonomy to Tibet. This is regrettable because, for most of history, Tibet was either highly autonomous or completely independent. China has declared that it alone would make the decisions on selecting the next Dalai Lama. What an outrageous interference in religion and freedom. China has encouraged the migration of Han Chinese in Tibetan areas. China continues its political crackdown on Tibet.

The State Department's 2016 Report on Human Rights Practices notes that the Chinese Government engaged in severe repression of Tibet's unique religious, cultural, and linguistic heritage. China has clamped down on the flow of information into and about Tibet. It imposed restrictive regulations on religious practices, censored Buddhist literature and information, and demolished Tibetan Buddhist sites, and placed monasteries under its control, and has imprisoned Tibetan prisoners of conscience.

One way in which Tibet has been illustrated for us is exemplified by Mr. Gere here, and that was the fine movie that was made. I am concerned that Chinese control and influence over media would make creating another movie difficult or impossible. Chinese interests are strongly involved in a large proportion of the movie screens in the United States. And, of course, China has this policy of only admitting a certain number of movies into China so they can punish any studio that they don't like in ways that North Korea could—well beyond anything North Korea tried to do to Sony. So to think that we allow China to exercise that kind of control while giving them free access to our markets is something Congress needs to review.

China has increased its military presence in Tibet and has built roads, airfields, and infrastructure that could be used to transport and support Chinese military forces repressing people in Tibet. This not only impacts the Tibetan population but also affects India. We are trying to build a strategic relationship and partnership with India, and we have got to commend India for providing refuge to over 90,000 Tibetans, including the Dalai Lama himself, who have had to flee Chinese repression.

Congress must act quickly to counter China's repressive tactics and policies toward Tibet. This is important for our own standing as leaders in the world's human rights. There are two bills before us this year. I would recommend that everyone on this subcommittee and on the full committee cosponsor both of them, the Reciprocal Access to Tibet Act of 2017, and Expressing the Sense of Congress with Respect to United States Policy Toward Tibet.

Looking at the second bill first, H. Con. Res. 89, introduced by our chairman along with myself, Ileana Ros-Lehtinen, and Ranking

Member Engel, asked the administration to make Tibet an important issue in U.S.-China relations to fully implement the Tibetan Policy Act of 2002 and to encourage China to engage in dialogue with the Dalai Lama or his representatives leading to a negotiated agreement with respect to Tibet.

The second bill is H.R. 1872, introduced by Congressman McGovern, which would deny Chinese Government officials access to the United States if they are responsible for restricting American journalists and American diplomats from traveling to Tibet.

In 2008, when China's military crackdown on Tibetans occurred, I was pleased that this House voted overwhelmingly for House Resolution 1077, calling upon the Chinese Government to end its crackdown in Tibet and to begin substantive dialogue with the people and the leaders of Tibet. It is disheartening to see that, in the 9 years since, China's suppression of Tibet has increased.

And a few months ago, in June, I had the pleasure of talking to Mr. Gere about Tibet. I look forward to hearing from him, Mr. Gershman, and Mr. Tethong on how Congress can support the Tibetan people at this important time.

And I yield back.

Mr. YOHO. Thank you, sir.

Now we will go to opening statements by members.

Mr. Chabot?

Mr. CHABOT. Thank you, Mr. Chairman, for holding this important hearing and very timely.

China's decades-long oppression of Tibet is a constant example of the PRC's total disregard for religious freedom and human decency. Just this past weekend, another Tibetan monk set himself on fire to protest China's ongoing tyranny. China has systematically marginalized Tibet for over 50 years now, and I want to commend Mr. Gere for being a leader on this issue for such a long time, having met and heard him testify a number of times here.

And thank you for sticking with it over the years. We really appreciate that.

China has reneged on their commitment to allow Tibet to operate as an autonomous region and failed to guarantee its people their personal and religious freedoms. Unfortunately, China's crackdown on Tibetans has consistently increased in recent years resulting in numerous violent clashes and the death of many innocent people. I am deeply concerned that China's growing global assertiveness puts the future of Tibet and the Tibetan people at an even greater risk. I believe that Tibet's struggle for autonomy and religious freedom could be in real jeopardy. That is why my colleagues and I must continue to demonstrate to the global community that the human rights of the Tibetan people must be respected by China.

U.S. officials should implore China to do everything we possibly can to engage in meaningful and constructive dialogue with the Dalai Lama to reach a long-term solution that results in enduring peace. So I look forward to the panel and yield back.

Mr. YOHO. Thank you, sir.

Next, we will go to Ms. Ros-Lehtinen, chairman emeritus, from Florida.

Ms. ROS-LEHTINEN. Thank you so much, Chairman Yoho, and thank you to Ranking Member—we have got a private joke going here—stop it, Ted—Sherman for this meeting.

Tibet is an issue that is near and dear to my heart, and I want to thank both you and Ranking Member Sherman for allowing me to join your subcommittee and hear from our distinguished panelists. It has been a privilege to work closely on these issues with both Carl and Richard. I like to name drop, you know, first-name basis.

I want to thank Mr. Gere for taking the time to be with us today and to wait so long—but we had votes—and then have to hear from us yet again. But you have been a staunch defender and advocate, a tireless worker on behalf of the Tibetan people.

A little over 10 years ago, I authored a bill alongside our departed pal, Tom Lantos—and I want to thank him for his work on this—which eventually became law, that recognized His Holiness the Dalai Lama with our highest honor, the Congressional Gold Medal, showing the world that we stand with the people of Tibet in their struggle for freedom. But in the years since, Mr. Chairman, I have been increasingly worried that Tibet has been pushed to the periphery of U.S. foreign policy. Beijing's repressive policies in Tibet have only been getting worse with additional travel restrictions against Tibetans and U.S. citizens, restrictive regulations on religious affairs, and censorship of Buddhist literature and information. We are also seeing Beijing demolish Tibetan Buddhist sites, jailing more Tibetan prisoners of conscience, and declaring that it, Beijing, has the decisionmaking power over the reincarnation of the Dalai Lama.

Sadly, instead of supporting the people of Tibet and standing up to Beijing's policy, U.S. administration after U.S. administration has held back being fearful of upsetting the Chinese, and this is simply unacceptable. We must stand strong in our commitment to the people of Tibet, and that is why, last month, I was proud to introduce House Concurrent Resolution 89, alongside Ranking Member Engel, Chairman Yoho, Ranking Member Sherman, and Steve Chabot, and our bill outlines a path forward on U.S. policy on Tibet. And I urge my colleagues to cosponsor this important bipartisan resolution. It details certain priorities, including pressing Beijing to enter into a dialogue with the Dalai Lama that leads to a negotiated agreement on Tibet, and it publicly calls for the immediate release of political and religious prisoners. It calls for the appointment of a Special Coordinator for Tibetan Issues and at the State Department who would report directly to the Secretary of State. It calls for the revocation of appropriate privileges of any Chinese officials responsible for impeding access of U.S. citizens to Tibet, an issue that I am also proud to be working on as a cosponsor of my good friend Jim McGovern and his bill, the Reciprocal Access to Tibet Act, H.R. 1872. I urge my colleagues to cosponsor this important legislation as well. All of the Chinese regime's actions that I mentioned are not only immoral and unjust, but they violate the Tibetan people's most basic human rights, and they are threatening the stability of a crucial area for U.S. interest. Our own U.S. national security interests dictate that we oppose China's increasingly repressive policies on Tibet and that we work toward a negotiated solution and start making the treatment of the people of Tibet an important factor in our relations with Beijing. So thank you, Chairman Yoho. Thank you, Ranking Member Sherman, for taking the time. And I look forward to hearing from our distinguished panelists.

I yield back. Thank you sir.

Mr. YOHO. Thank you for your comments.

And I would like to ask if there is no objection to allowing Mr. McGovern, the author of the Reciprocal Access to Tibet Act of 2017, to say a few words.

Hearing no objection, Mr. McGovern.

Mr. McGOVERN. Whew, thank you.

I want to thank Chairman Yoho and Ranking Member Sherman for convening this hearing, and I want to thank my colleagues up here. And I hope the Chinese Government is listening because in a Congress where there is lots that divides Democrats and Republicans, this is an issue that brings us together. We are all speaking with one voice here today. We are all saying that Tibet is important, that human rights in Tibet is important, and that we believe our Government must do more. And I think this is a particularly important time because the human rights situation in Tibet is dire and deteriorating. And I gotta be honest with you: I am frustrated that our Government hasn't done more over the years. I say that not only in reference to the Trump administration; I, quite frankly, was frustrated while President Obama was in office that, while some symbolic steps were taken, in the end, Tibet's status remained the same. And so, whether it was Democratic or Republican administrations, we haven't done nearly enough to raise this issue.

There was no progress—there has been no progress in restarting the Tibet and Chinese dialogue or advancing Tibetan autonomy. Control over the practice of Buddhism tightened. And the use of the Tibetan language has become more restrictive. And too many people found the situation so unbearable that they took to the unimaginable decision to self-immolate. As things have worsened in recent years, there have been no consequences for Chinese authorities, none.

All of us love and respect His Holiness the Dalai Lama, and that is as it should be. Our relationship with him and our solidarity helped keep the Tibet issue in the public eye. But that is not enough. The Dalai Lama is 82 years old, and he is getting tired. For that reason he recently decided to turn over his international engagements to emissaries. I believe the Dalai Lama could play a very constructive role in negotiating a better future for the Tibetan people, but China clearly doesn't see it that way. China is waiting him out and counting on his eventual departure to remove Tibet from the international agenda.

So we need to move now, and we need some leverage. And that is why, earlier this year, along with a bipartisan group of members, I introduced H.R. 1872, the Reciprocal Access to Tibet Act. As has been mentioned, this bill imposes consequences for just one aspect of China's bad behavior: Its restrictions on travel to areas in China where ethnic Tibetans live. Chinese diplomats have unrestrictive access to anywhere in the United States. U.S. citizens and U.S.

journalists and U.S. diplomats ought to have the same. And the current status of things, quite frankly, is unacceptable. If China wants its citizens and officials to travel freely in the United States, Americans must be able to travel freely in China, including Tibet. But allowing travel to Tibet is only one step China needs to take, and there are others. Most, especially China, should permit His Holiness the Dalai Lama to return to Tibet for a visit if he so desires. He has that right, and he must have that opportunity before it is too late.

On our side, we need to insist that the State Department name a Special Coordinator for Tibetan Issues. This appointment is a statutory requirement. To make progress on Tibet issues, we need someone in charge. We in Congress should also insist that the administration make use of the global Magnitsky Act to sanction Chinese officials responsible for torture and extrajudicial killings of Tibetans, like the revered monk Tenzin Delek Rinpoche. It has been nearly 2½ years since he died in a Chinese prison, and still there is no accountability for his death. I say to all of you as my colleagues: Time may be running out for the Tibetan people. All those who say they believe in the rights of the Tibetans must move beyond words to concrete actions. We have been talking the talk for years. We now need to walk the walk. If human rights on Tibet really matters, then our Government, the United States Government, has to stop being such a cheap date when it comes to this issue. We need a bolder policy. We need to be thinking out of the box, and we need to indicate to the Chinese Government that we are serious on this matter. Let us take advantage of our power, let us create some leverage. The first step could be a markup and the passage of H.R. 1872 and the other legislation that has been mentioned here.

But I will close with this: I have always believed that if the United States stands for anything, we need to stand out loud and foursquare for human rights, and what is happening to the Tibetan people and the Tibetan culture is unconscionable. And it is no longer enough for us to tell people we revere the Dalai Lama or meet him when he comes here, although that is important. Now is the time to take the next steps. I want a good relationship with China. I admire the Chinese people, but this is a serious human rights matter, and it demands more serious attention by our Government.

And, again, I thank the chairman and the ranking member for convening this hearing. I yield back.

Mr. YOHO. Thank you for your comments, and we will get on with the—go ahead. We will go on to the testimony from our esteemed panel. And I feel blessed that we have you three experts here today. Not only are you experts in the area, your passion and your persistence is so important in getting this message out to bring the spotlight on the world's stage.

We have with us Mr. Richard Gere—I think everybody knows or has seen his movies—chair of the Board of Directors of the International Campaign for Tibet; Mr. Tenzin Tethong, director of Tibetan Service for Radio Free Asia; and Mr. Carl Gershman, president of the National Endowment for Democracy.

And you guys probably have done this more than I have. You know there will be a 5-minute timer in front of you. Press your button that says "talk" so the microphone is on, and then you will see the lights go from green, yellow, and red, and we will let you talk.

And, Mr. Gere, if you would start off. Thank you.

STATEMENT OF MR. RICHARD GERE, CHAIR OF THE BOARD OF DIRECTORS, INTERNATIONAL CAMPAIGN FOR TIBET

Mr. GERE. Well, first of all, I am going to be incredibly blunt with you: I am totally knocked out by the words that I am hearing from all of you. And I have seen this evolve over decades now, how people talk about Tibet and from what part of their being they speak. And this is coming from a deep place in all of you. I think everyone in this room is feeling this from a deep place, how important this is, maybe not strategically but humanly, and what it means to us as Americans to be coming from this place of universal responsibility protecting the welfare and human rights of everyone on this planet.

But I really want to thank you, Chairman Yoho, for presiding over this.

Mr. Sherman, thank you very much.

And, of course, Ileana, we are on a first-name basis.

And, Eddie, thank you very much for pushing so hard.

Chairman, as always, thank you for the depth of perception and the openness of your emotions in dealing with a subject as difficult as this.

I also see, over to my right, there is a painting up here of Tom Lantos, and as you know, he was chairman of this committee. He was also the convener of the Congressional Human Rights Caucus. He was a great friend of mine, great friend of the Tibetan people, and a close and dear friend of His Holiness the Dalai Lama. I think he would be so happy right now as he is looking down from there to hear these fiery, compassionate, and deeply committed words from all of you, and I thank you for that.

Fifteen years ago, something kind of miraculous happened. At the end of 2002, President Bush signed into law the Tibetan Policy Act after it received bipartisan support in both the House and the Senate. This legislation dictates how U.S. policy toward Tibet should be conducted by the administration. Congress and this subcommittee have a very important role to play in monitoring that policy and how it is to be conducted. Ten years ago, on October 17th, 2007, the U.S. Congress bestowed upon His Holiness our highest civilian honor here in America with the awarding of the Congressional Gold Medal, and clearly, there are people in this room who worked really hard on that to make that happen. I want to thank all of you again for having done that.

There were so many wonderful people there that day, the entire government, and it was bipartisan at the highest levels of President Bush, and First Lady Laura Bush was there. Mr. Boehner was there. Nancy Pelosi, Mitch McConnell. And I actually remember Mitch McConnell giving the most powerful speech that evening on human rights and on behalf of His Holiness the Dalai Lama. It makes me kind of wish that people would be talking today the way they did then on how important human rights are.

As Americans, as people who care, it is kind of the centerpiece of the American soul, is that we do care, and we have to continually talk about these things and express them.

Tibet has been an issue that has earned extraordinary support in the U.S. Congress over the decades, including humanitarian aid for the Tibetan refugee communities in India and Nepal. The congressional delegation led by Leader Pelosi and Congressman Sensenbrenner, which visited India and Nepal last May, confirmed once again the commitment of this institution to Tibet and saw firsthand the positive impact that development aid has had in these communities, and it is pretty extraordinary, something to be very proud of. Since the 1990s, subsequent U.S. administrations and Presidents have supported the call of His Holiness the Dalai Lama, not for independence but for genuine autonomy for the Tibetan people as guaranteed in the Chinese Constitution, and for China to respect the distinct identity of the Tibetan people, including their language, their religion, and their culture, and to stop the ongoing persecution of Tibetans.

The respect for the identity of a people and their religion is something that the American people understand very well and deeply care about. Before being politicians or actors, we are human beings who understand that oppression cannot be tolerated. We understand that all human beings have the right to the pursuit of happiness and to avoid suffering. This is what His Holiness the Dalai Lama continuously reminds us of: To look at what unites us as human beings, as compassionate people sharing our time and space on this small and very beautiful planet drifting through an endless universe. We are in this together, all of us.

This is consistent in this message that His Holiness and our Tibetan brothers and sisters send to the Chinese Government and to all of us. Despite the historical, cultural, linguistic, and ethnic differences, and despite decades of oppression, the proposal for genuine autonomy presented by the Tibetans shows a path toward peaceful coexistence and away from endless conflict. Despite these efforts, the Chinese Government ceased formal talks with the representatives of His Holiness the Dalai Lama in 2010, and Tibetans inside Tibet continued to live in very, very challenging times indeed.

Just last week, November 26th, a 63-year-old Tibetan monk named Tenga self-immolated in Tibet. He was the 151st Tibetan to self-immolate in the land of snow since the first one in 2009. We actually have a picture of him right now.

Do you have that?

Ladies and gentlemen, this is Tenga, who just sacrificed his life for the Tibetan people, his brothers and sisters. But not just that, I think it was a message to us and perhaps our failure to engage an issue which is literally life and death for the Tibetan people and their culture. I don't know if you can put this on the record. It is up there. Okay. Good. Thank you.

According to our sources, the body of Tenga has not been returned to his family. This seems to be what the Chinese authorities are doing now. They either allow prisoners to die, as Tenzin Delek Rinpoche, and then some are, in fact, tortured to death, and the bodies are not returned to their families. There is a collective punishment to the villages, to the families. This is clearly against international law, but it is carried out every day against Tibetans by the Chinese Government.

As we meet today, hundreds of Tibetans are imprisoned for expressing their opinions or beliefs. Tibetan monasteries across Tibet are under strict police surveillance with police stations actually built inside the monasteries or sometimes just besides them. Religious regulations give the Chinese Communist Party, not Tibetan Buddhists, the authority to identify and appoint reincarnated Tibetan lamas, including the Dalai Lama. Tibetan nomads are being removed from their land and relocated in socialist villages. A number of urban centers in Tibet now have a majority of ethnic Han Chinese settlers, and the use of a Tibetan language is intensely discouraged. These are the policies that threaten the very survival of Tibetan identity.

Now, just a few weeks ago, as you know, the 19th Congress of the Communist Party reaffirmed and expanded the power and role of President Xi Jinping. As China's profile obviously grows on the world's stage, its accountability as to international law and norms must also grow. The United States leadership in this area has always been essential to that accountability, and I call on this committee and our Government to make sure that accountability is robust.

During President Trump's recent visit to China, the White House stated that the issue of human rights was raised with Chinese authorities. We don't have the details on that, unfortunately, what was said. While this is good, President Trump and Secretary Tillerson did not publicly highlight the lack of respect of human rights in Tibet or the need for China to restart the dialogue process with the Dalai Lama. Now, this is out of line completely with the provisions of the Tibetan Policy Act.

It is now critical that the U.S. Congress takes concrete initiatives to make sure that the Tibet Policy Act, which is law, is fully implemented and that China is consistently reminded that the U.S. stands with the Tibetan people in full support of their peaceful aspirations.

Earlier this year, Congressman McGovern and Senator Rubio introduced legislation in the House and the Senate to put pressure on China to allow U.S. diplomats, journalists, and NGOs to have free access to Tibet based on the principle of reciprocity. U.S. citizens face severe restrictions in their access to Tibet, while Chinese citizens, diplomats, NGOs, journalists, and media have free access to the United States. By the way, I have not been allowed in mainland China since 1993.

Reciprocity is an important principle in diplomatic relations that should be implemented, not only when it comes to trade but also to freedom of movement and freedom of information. To give you a few examples of the lack of reciprocity with China, the State Department reports that the officials of the Government of the United States submitted 39 requests for diplomatic access to the Tibetan Autonomous Region, TAR, between May 2011 and July 2015. Only 4 were granted of the 39. And when such requests are granted, diplomatic personnel are closely supervised and given few opportunities to meet with local residents not approved by the authorities.

And those that were on the codel to Tibet know how monitored they were in this process. It was extremely difficult, impossible, to meet anyone without supervision.

In September 2016, an article in the Washington Post reported that: "The Tibetan Autonomous Region is harder to visit as a journalist than North Korea."

Furthermore, foreign correspondents——

Mr. YOHO. Mr. Gere, sorry. Can I get you to hold your recommendations so we can get to the other witnesses? And I hate to ask you that because you waited for us for 45 minutes.

Mr. GERE. Absolutely. No, please.

Mr. YOHO. But I will give you time during my questioning to finish that up.

Mr. GERE. No, that is fine. That is perfectly fine. This is your show.

[The prepared statement of Mr. Gere follows:]

House Foreign Affairs Subcommittee on Asia

Hearing on "U.S. Policy towards Tibet: Access, Religious Freedom, and Human
Rights."
December 6, 2017

Testimony by Mr. Richard Gere
Chairman, International Campaign for Tibet

Chairman Yoho, Ranking Member Sherman, Chairman Emeritus Ros-Lehtinen,

Let me first of all thank you for inviting me to testify before the Asia Subcommittee
on the topic of "US Policy towards Tibet." This is a timely initiative as the situation
inside Tibet continues to be critical and needs the full support of the US Congress.

As I look on the wall of this Committee, I can see the portrait of the late
Congressman and Chairman of this Committee, Tom Lantos, a dear friend of the
Tibetan people and of His Holiness the Dalai Lama, who was the first Member of
Congress to invite His Holiness to speak on Capitol Hill more than 30 years ago.
Chairman Yoho, by convening this hearing you are honoring the legacy of a hero of
our time, a kind and fearless man.

15 years ago, at the end of 2002, President Bush signed into law the Tibetan Policy
Act, after it received bipartisan support in both the House and the Senate. This
legislation dictates how US policy towards Tibet should be conducted by the
Administration. Congress and this Sub-Committee have a very important role to
play in monitoring that.

10 years ago, on October 17, 2007, the US Congress bestowed upon His Holiness the
Highest Civilian Honor with the awarding of the Congressional Gold Medal; I can see
in this room some of the people who worked so hard to make this happen- thank
you! On that special day in the Capitol Rotunda, you were also joined by President
Bush and First Lady Laura Bush.

Tibet is an issue that has garnered extraordinary support in the US Congress over
the decades, including humanitarian aid for the Tibetan refugee communities in
India and Nepal. The Congressional delegation led by Leader Pelosi and
Congressman Sensenbrenner, which visited India and Nepal last May, confirmed
once again the commitment of this institution to Tibet and saw first-hand the
positive impact that development aid had for these communities.

Since the nineties, subsequent US Administrations and Presidents have supported
the call of His Holiness the Dalai Lama for genuine autonomy for the Tibetan people
and have called on China to respect the distinct identity of the Tibetan people;

including their language, their religion and their culture, and to stop the persecution of Tibetans.

The respect for the identity of a people, of their religion, is something the American people understand very well. Before being politicians, you are human beings who understand that oppression cannot be tolerated; you understand that all human beings have the right to the pursuit of happiness. This is what His Holiness the Dalai Lama continuously reminds us; to look at what unites us as human beings, not what divides us.

This is the message that His Holiness and the Tibetans continue to send to the Chinese government. Despite the historical, cultural, linguistic and ethnic differences, and despite decades of oppression, the proposal for genuine autonomy presented by the Tibetans shows a path towards coexistence, and away from conflict.

Despite these efforts, the Chinese government ceased formal talks with the representatives of His Holiness the Dalai Lama in 2010, and Tibetans inside Tibet live in very challenging times.

Just last week, on November 26, a 63-year-old Tibetan monk named Tenga self-immolated in Tibet. He was the 151st Tibetan to self-immolate in the Land of Snows since 2009. This is his picture. Even sending a picture like this abroad can, and has, cost Tibetan men and women their freedom and resulted in lengthy prison sentences.

According to our sources, the body of Tenga has not yet been returned to his family members, who have been put under police surveillance.

As we meet today, hundreds of Tibetans are imprisoned for expressing their opinions or beliefs; Buddhist monasteries across Tibet are under strict police surveillance, with police stations built inside or besides them; religious regulations give the Chinese Communist Party – not Tibetan Buddhists - the authority to identify and appoint reincarnated Tibetan Lamas, including the Dalai Lama; Tibetan nomads are being removed from their land and relocated in "socialist villages"; a number of urban centers in Tibet now have a majority ethnic Chinese population; and the use of the Tibetan language is discouraged. This threatens the Tibetan language to being reduced to a colloquial use only.

These are the policies that threaten the very survival of Tibetan identity.

Just few weeks ago, the Nineteenth Congress of the Communist Party reaffirmed President Xi's role. As China's role grows on the world stage, its accountability on conforming to international law and norms must also grow, and the United States has an essential role to play in making that happen.

During President Trump's recent visit to China, the White House stated that the issue of human rights was raised with Chinese authorities. While this is good, President Trump and Secretary Tillerson did not publicly highlight the lack of respect of human rights in Tibet or the need for China to restart the dialogue process with the Dalai Lama; this is out of line with the provisions of the Tibetan Policy Act[1].

It is now critical that the US Congress takes concrete initiatives to make sure that the Tibetan Policy Act is fully implemented and that China understands that the US stands with the Tibetan people.

Earlier this year Congressman McGovern and Senator Rubio introduced legislation in the House and in the Senate to put pressure on China to allow US diplomats, journalists, and NGOs to have free access to Tibet based on the principle of reciprocity. US citizens face severe restrictions in their access to Tibet, while Chinese citizens, diplomats, NGOs journalists and media have free access to the United States.

Reciprocity is an important principle in diplomatic relations that should be implemented not only when it comes to trade, but also to freedom of movement and freedom of information.

Just to give you few examples of the lack of reciprocity with China, the State Department reports that "officials of the Government of the United States submitted 39 requests for diplomatic access to the Tibet Autonomous Region between May 2011 and July 2015, but only four were granted; and when such requests are granted, diplomatic personnel are closely supervised and given few opportunities to meet local residents not approved by authorities."

A September 2016 article in the Washington Post reported that "The Tibet Autonomous Region . . . is harder to visit as a journalist than North Korea."

Furthermore the Foreign Correspondents Club of China reports that:

---

[1] According to the Tibetan Polciy Act of 2002
SEC. 613. TIBET NEGOTIATIONS.
(a) POLICY-
(1) IN GENERAL- The President and the Secretary should encourage the Government of the People's Republic of China to enter into a dialogue with the Dalai Lama or his representatives leading to a negotiated agreement on Tibet.
SEC. 617. RELEASE OF PRISONERS AND ACCESS TO PRISONS.
The President and the Secretary, in meetings with representatives of the Government of the People's Republic of China, should-
(1) request the immediate and unconditional release of all those held prisoner for expressing their political or religious views in Tibet;
(2) seek access for international humanitarian organizations to prisoners in Tibet to ensure that prisoners are not being mistreated and are receiving necessary medical care; and
(3) seek the immediate medical parole of Tibetan prisoners known to be in serious ill health.

A) 2008 rules prevent foreign reporters from visiting the Tibet Autonomous Region without prior permission from the Government of such Region;

(B) such permission has only rarely been granted; and

(C) although the 2008 rules allow journalists to travel freely in other parts of China, Tibetan areas outside such Region remain "effectively off-limits to foreign reporters".

The Department of State reports that in addition to having to obtain permission to enter the Tibet Autonomous Region, foreign tourists—

(A) must be accompanied at all times by a government-designated tour guide;

(B) are rarely granted permission to enter the region by road;

(C) are largely barred from visiting around the March anniversary of a 1959 Tibetan uprising; and

(D) are banned from visiting the area where Larung Gar, the world's largest center for the study of Tibetan Buddhism, and the site of a large-scale campaign to expel students and demolish living quarters, is located.

Mr. Chairman, I would like to make the following recommendations, which I hope you can endorse today with the consent of the Committee:

Recommendations

- Given the deteriorating situation in Tibet and the Chinese unwillingness to address the genuine grievances of the Tibetan people, the Congress should send a strong message by passing the bipartisan Bill, H.R.1872 —Reciprocal Access to Tibet Act of 2017 to promote access for American citizens, diplomats and journalists in Tibet similar to that enjoyed by Chinese citizens, diplomats and journalists in the United States;

- It should pass the bipartisan resolution H.Con.Res.89 - Expressing the sense of Congress with respect to United States policy toward Tibet and that the treatment of the Tibetan people should be an important factor in the conduct of United States relations with the People's Republic of China.

- Ask the Administration to elevate the issue of Tibet to an important factor in bilateral relations with the People's Republic of China;

- Ask the Administration to use economic and political leverage to pressure China to respect Tibet's distinct religion and culture and to resume negotiations with envoys of the Dalai Lama on solving the Tibet problem;

- Urge the Administration to work with the European Union and other countries to formulate a multilateral approach to the Tibet issue.

- Urge the early designation of the US Special Coordinator for Tibetan Issues in the State Department;

- Ask American diplomats, including representatives of multilateral organizations, to seek access to Tibetan areas based on the spirit of principle of reciprocity by which Chinese diplomats and journalists enjoy unrestricted access in the United States.

- Ask for a report from the State Department on how many requests for diplomatic access to Tibet has been made to the Chinese authorities in 2017;

- Ask Secretary Rex Tillerson to meet the Dalai Lama to get a first-hand information on the situation of the Tibetan people;

- Ask the Administration to raise Tibet in appropriate international fora, including U.N. bodies;

- Ask the Administration to continue humanitarian assistance to Tibetan refugees to preserve and promote their distinct identity and culture;

- Ask the Administration to vigorously pursue the United States' long-stated goal of establishing a consulate in Lhasa.

- Organize a Congressional/staff delegation to Tibet to assess the situation;

- Organize a Congressional/staff delegation to Dharamsala to assess the situation of the Tibetan community in exile;

- Recommend a US Commission on International Religious Freedom (USCIRF) delegation to China and Tibet to assess the state of religious freedom of the Tibetan people;

- Ask the Congressional Research Service (CRS) to do a report on the status of religious freedom in Tibet;

- Urge China to release Tibetan political prisoners, including the 11th Panchen Lama, Gedhun Choekyi Nyima;

- Urge the new Chinese leadership to re-evaluate the 'stability maintenance' approach applied in Tibet and the dominance of the security apparatus.

Thank you.

Mr. YOHO. And the show must go on.

Thank you for all that, though, because I want to hear the rest of that, and you have got some great recommendations I think everybody should hear.

Mr. Tethong.

STATEMENT OF MR. TENZIN TETHONG, DIRECTOR OF THE TIBETAN SERVICE, RADIO FREE ASIA

Mr. TETHONG. First of all, I would like to begin by thanking Chairman Yoho and Ranking Member Sherman for this opportunity to testify at this hearing. In consideration of time limits, I will go over only some of the main points in my written statement, which has already been submitted.

As director or of the Tibetan Service at Radio Free Asia, I would like to focus my comments on the challenges we face as a news organization of getting news from the region and fulfilling our mandated mission of bringing this news to the Tibetan people. It is extremely difficult for any of our journalists to have normal access to Tibet. Nevertheless, many of them maintain various levels of contact with networks of trusted sources inside Tibet who can provide tips, leads, images, video, and confirmation of events.

During President Xi Jinping's tenure, China has grown more strident in enforcing a comprehensive censorship and propaganda operation in Tibet and increased attacks on Tibetan culture by demolishing holy sites and demonizing the spiritual leader of the Tibetan people, His Holiness the Dalai Lama.

Last week, as Richard has already mentioned, RFA reported the 151st self-immolation protest since 2009. It was carried out by a 63-year-old monk from Kardze who called out for freedom in Tibet before he set himself aflame. These self-immolation protests have explicitly called for greater freedom for the Tibetan people and the swift return of His Holiness the Dalai Lama to Tibet.

But each time such a protest takes place, authorities intensify efforts to clamp down on the sharing of information, and entire regions and prefectures can be plunged into communication darkness in the wake of such protests. Weibo and WeChat, the dominant social media platforms in China, are heavily monitored and restricted. This was especially evident in the lead-up to the recent 19th Party Congress. Authorities ramped up efforts to police WeChat and warned Tibetan monastery heads about the severe consequences the entire establishments would face if monks and nuns shared or discussed content deemed sensitive.

Chinese authorities also bring the heavy hand of law enforcement down on any Tibetan caught sharing information of events with foreign outlets. Authorities harass families of reporters and stringers working for Radio Free Asia, and they have even targeted Tibetans in the United States. A Tibetan American in New York, a regular listener to RFA who sends our programs out over social media, was somehow identified by Chinese security authorities. The authorities tracked down his family in Tibet, interrogating and threatening them with retribution.

While the Chinese journalists travel and work freely in the United States, no RFA Tibetan reporter can obtain a journalist visa to enter Tibet. Even when applying for visas to visit family, RFA reporters are subject to extensive questioning by Chinese Embassy officials while parallel inquiries are made of family members back home by local authorities.

Such a process can go on indefinitely and more often than not result in a denial. Two months ago, one of our reporters was granted permission to visit his ailing brother after weeks of pleading for a visa and was finally able to visit and spend the last few days with his brother before he passed away.

Another reporter who had not met his family members for 10 years had to rendezvous in Hong Kong because he was repeatedly denied a visa to visit home. Yet another who wanted to visit relatives in China on a 72-hour nonvisa requirement transit privilege accorded to all U.S. passport holders was denied entry because he was identified as a Tibetan.

Beijing has recently redirected increased resources to build up its Tibetan language media operations on radio, online, and TV, which offers audiences almost solely entertainment programming punctuated by propaganda-driven news serving the CCP's narrative. All the while, they continue to try and deny access to RFA's programming on radio and online by jamming shortwave signals and blocking access to the Tibetan Web site.

The erosion of religious and—pardon me, I have just one more paragraph—the erosion of religious rights and freedoms in Tibet may be best illustrated by the demolition and crackdown on Larung Gar this year. Larung Gar is one of the most prominent and vibrant Tibetan Buddhist learning centers with monks and nuns from all over the country. We were able to cover these developments because many of his residents sent us photos, reports, and videos. While, similarly, last year, local activists in eastern Tibet informed us of mining activities in the region that was causing extensive environmental damage. When the mining was finally halted, the local Tibetans informed us that it was outside attention, especially the steady reporting of RFA which forced Chinese authorities to put an end to the mining.

Trust is a two-way street for RFA reporter sources and audiences. We recently learned of a monk was among those expelled from Larung Gar. He told us that he was devastated when he was expelled, but he had no regrets in reaching out to us. Such feedback reaffirms the importance of our mission. As one Tibetan listener inside China recently said: "RFA broadcasts clearly about the conditions inside Tibet and where His Holiness the Dalai Lama is going to visit and what he is doing. Because they broadcast such true information, I strongly trust it." RFA strives to keep earning that trust and keep connecting the Tibetan people with the truth. Thank you.

[The prepared statement of Mr. Tethong follows:]

Testimony of Tenzin Tethong
Director of the Tibetan Service, Radio Free Asia
Asia and the Pacific Subcommittee, House Foreign Affairs Committee
December 6, 2017
"U.S. Policy Toward Tibet: Access Religious Freedom, and Human Rights"

First, I would like to thank Representatives Ted Yoho and Brad Sherman for this opportunity to testify today at this hearing on "U.S. Policy Toward Tibet: Access Religious Freedom, and Human Rights." As Director of the Tibetan Service at Radio Free Asia, I would like to focus my comments on the challenges we face as a news organization of getting news from the region and fulfilling our congressionally mandated mission of bringing this news to the Tibetan people. It's extremely difficult for any of our journalists to have normal access to Tibet, which ranks among the world's worst media environments after North Korea. Nevertheless, many of them maintain various levels of contact with vast networks of trusted sources inside who can provide tips, leads, images, video, and confirmation of events.

Radio Free Asia's Tibetan Service has had to double its efforts to meet the increasing challenges of bringing the Tibetan people reliable, timely news and information. During President Xi Jinping's tenure, China has grown even more strident in enforcing a comprehensive censorship and propaganda operation in Tibet. These tactics are designed to keep the Tibetans in the dark as Beijing has stepped up its suppression of Tibetan identity and religious freedom, continued to seize land and mineral wealth from Tibetan-populated areas in China, and increased its attacks on Tibetan cultural heritage by demolishing holy sites and demonizing the Tibetan people's spiritual leader, the Dalai Lama.

On any given day, people in Tibet may wake up without access to the Internet and unable to make a phone call because authorities have shut down all communications. Tibetans can find themselves stopped and searched randomly at roadside security checkpoints, their phones and electronic devices confiscated to be probed for sensitive images, like those of the Dalai Lama. Nuns and monks from nearby monasteries may be rounded up by police to be detained or warned about the use of social media. And entire families may be taken into custody under suspicion that one individual, or a close relative, has communicated with foreign media or NGOs.

Beijing has always kept a tight lid on Tibet, mostly to conceal the extent of its abuses stemming from its policies in the region. In 2008 an uprising in Lhasa spread throughout all Tibetan regions within China, culminating in the last protests leading up to the Beijing Olympics. In recent years, there has been a new form of protest by way of self-immolations against Beijing's rule. Last week, RFA reported the 151st self-immolation protest since the current wave began in 2009. It was carried out by a 63-year-old monk from Kardze who called out for freedom in Tibet before he set himself aflame. These self-immolation protests have explicitly called for greater freedom for the Tibetan people and the swift return of the Dalai Lama to Tibet. They represent the deep frustrations and yearnings of the Tibetan people. But each time such a protest takes place, authorities intensify efforts to clamp down on the sharing of information. Entire prefectures and regions can be plunged into communications darkness in the wake of such protests as messaging apps like WeChat are shut down, along with the Internet and phone lines.

Virtually all expressions of Tibetan identity – including the practice of religion and the teaching of the Tibetan language -- online and on social media are filtered, monitored or outright censored. Those who are considered to have violated what's deemed necessary by authorities to preserve stability often suffer severe consequences such as jailing and torture. Facebook and YouTube are blocked, and Chinese telecoms that control Chinese Internet access have been ordered by the state to ban the use of VPNs – removing nearly any possibility for Tibetans to access sensitive content on outside social media and websites. China's vast system of Internet filters and blocks, known collectively as "The Great Firewall," is tightly enforced in the Tibetan regions – where all online access and the Internet can be shut down at any given moment. Chinese state-sponsored hackers target the Tibetan diaspora and organizations outside China, using malware attacks to shut down overseas servers and IT infrastructure.

Weibo and WeChat, the dominant social media platforms in China, are heavily monitored and restricted. Tibetans who use WeChat to keep in touch with family and friends, but also to discuss sensitive topics in created groups, risk harassment and jail. RFA recently reported how Chinese authorities have begun to infiltrate these groups to monitor and crack down on individuals. This was especially evident in the lead-up to the recent 19th Party Congress. Authorities ramped up efforts to police WeChat and warn Tibetan monastery heads about the severe consequences their entire establishments would face if monks and nuns shared or discussed content deemed sensitive. These measures follow on authorities tearing down satellite dishes on Tibetan homes in Qinghai and Sichuan to prevent access to RFA and VOA radio transmissions.

Chinese authorities have also severely limited access to foreign media sending correspondents to the Tibetan regions, despite assurances in 2015 that this could happen. The few correspondents who obtain permission are allowed to visit only under the condition of being under the constant supervision of state security handlers – making the region, in one *Washington Post* reporter's estimation, as cut off to foreign outlets as North Korea.

Chinese authorities also bring the heavy hand of law enforcement down on any Tibetan caught sharing information of events inside the Tibetan regions with foreign outlets. And their far-reaching efforts to stop the free flow of information extend well beyond the borders of China. Authorities harass Tibet-based families of reporters and stringers working for Radio Free Asia in Washington, D.C., as well as in Nepal and India. Chinese authorities even target Tibetans using WeChat and WhatsApp in the United States. A Tibetan-American in New York, a regular listener to RFA who re-sends our programs out over social media, was somehow identified by Chinese security authorities. Authorities tracked down his family in Tibet, interrogating and threatening them with retribution.

While Chinese journalists travel and work freely in the United States, no RFA Tibetan reporter can obtain a journalist's visa to enter Tibet. Even when applying for visas to visit family, RFA Tibetan reporters are subjected to extensive questioning by Chinese embassy officials, while parallel inquiries are made of family members back home by local authorities. Such a process can go on indefinitely, and, more often than not, results in a denial. Two months ago, one of our reporters was granted permission to visit his ailing brother after weeks of pleading for a visa, and was finally able to visit and spend the last few days with his brother before he passed away. Another reporter, who had not met his family members for 10 years, had to rendezvous in Hong

Kong because he was repeatedly denied a visa to visit home. Yet another, who wanted to visit with relatives in China on a 72-hour, non-visa-requirement transit privilege accorded to all U.S. passport holders, was denied entry in August because he was identified as a Tibetan.

Beijing has recently directed increased resources to build up its state-sponsored Tibetan language media operations on radio, online, and TV, which offers audiences almost solely entertainment programming punctuated with propaganda-driven news updates serving the CCP's narrative. All the while, they continue to try to deny access to RFA's programming on radio and online by jamming shortwave signals and blocking access to RFA's Tibetan news website.

Despite these efforts, or maybe because of them, Radio Free Asia has earned the trust of many Tibetans inside China, who are essential to the effectiveness of RFA's journalism. These networks of cultivated inside sources enable the Tibetan Service to break news about events that would otherwise be ignored by or censored by China's state controlled media. RFA was the first to report on the accelerated destruction of Larung Gar, and broke the news about the vast majority of recent self-immolations. The Tibetan Service has also provided exclusive coverage on China's exploitation of mineral wealth and mining operations in the region, which have prompted large-scale protests. In reporting these developments in Tibet through the years, we have become a reliable conduit for citizen-journalists in Tibet who are keen to inform the rest of the world of what is happening in their country.

The erosion of religious rights and freedoms in Tibet may be best illustrated by the accelerated demolition and crackdown on Larung Gar this year. Larung Gar is one of the most prominent and vibrant Tibetan Buddhist learning centers with monks and nuns from all over the country. We reported the forced expulsions and the extensive demolition of living quarters by the authorities, and how any monk or nun not officially certified as local was immediately expelled. We were able to cover these developments at Larung Gar because many of its residents sent us reports, photos, and video. Similarly, the year before, local activists in eastern Tibet informed us of mining activities in their region that was causing extensive environmental damage. When the mining was finally halted, the local Tibetans informed us that it was outside attention, especially the steady reporting by RFA, which had forced Chinese authorities to acknowledge the environmental damage and put an end to the mining.

Trust is a two-way street for RFA with both our sources and audiences. We recently learned that a monk who was among our sources at Larung Gar was expelled from the center under suspicion of helping us. He told us that though he was devastated, he had no regrets. People are prepared and willing to take such great risks to inform RFA, so we can in turn inform the Tibetan people. Such feedback reaffirms the importance of our mission. As one Tibetan listener inside China recently said, "RFA broadcasts clearly about the conditions inside Tibet and where His Holiness the Dalai Lama is going to visit and what he is doing. Because they broadcast such true information, I strongly trust it." RFA strives to keep earning that trust and keep connecting the Tibetan people with the truth.

Mr. YOHO. Mr. Tethong, thank you, and I appreciate you talking about the RFA, how important that is.

Mr. Gershman.

STATEMENT OF MR. CARL GERSHMAN, PRESIDENT, NATIONAL ENDOWMENT FOR DEMOCRACY

Mr. GERSHMAN. Thank you, Chairman Yoho and Ranking Member Sherman, for the invitation to testify before the subcommittee on this important matter. It is great to be here today amongst so many friends.

I want to begin by noting an article that appeared last week in the Washington Post, by David Ignatius, that was provocatively entitled "China's Plan to Rule the World." The article referenced several reports commissioned by the Pentagon and the Air Force, one of which describes China's economic and military buildup as perhaps the most ambitious grand strategy undertaken by a single nation in modern times. The article describes several dimensions of this strategy, in particular the $1 trillion One Belt, One Road trade and infrastructure plan that dwarfs by some seven times the Marshall Plan in post-war Europe and that has the strategic intent of constructing a Chinese-led order in Eurasia.

The United States and many other countries have tended to take a benign view of China's policies because Xi Jinping tries to present himself to the world as a global citizen, and he does not indulge in the brazen behavior of Russia's Vladimir Putin.

In addition, the illusion still persists that the integration of China into the global economy and political order will moderate its behavior and encourage its internal liberalization. In fact, the threat posed by China to the world order has increased with its growing economic power, and repression is worse today than at any time since the death of Mao Zedong four decades ago.

Nowhere is this repression more cruel than in Tibet, where the Chinese Government is pursuing a policy that the Dalai Lama has called cultural genocide. In addition to the systematic effort to destroy the Tibetan religion, language, culture, and distinct national identity, China has flooded Tibet with Han Chinese settlers, placed monasteries under direct government control, arrested and tortured writers, and forcibly resettled more than 2 million nomads in urban areas, destroying their traditional way of life and disrupting the fragile ecosystem of the Tibetan Plateau.

The death and likely murder in prison in July 2015 of Tenzin Delek Rinpoche, the beloved community leader and spiritual teacher, is emblematic of this oppression, which has led to the self-immolation and desperate protest of more than 150 Tibetans. The continued Tibetan resistance to Chinese oppression exposes the falseness of China's claim to the legitimacy of its rule in Tibet, which rests on the assertion stated in a white paper issued by the Chinese Government in 2015 that, "Tibet has been an integral part of China since antiquity." China insists that it won't resume negotiations over Tibet's status that it broke off in 2010 until the Dalai Lama agrees to this assertion, something he cannot do since it is contradicted by the historical literature and overlooks the fact that Communist China invaded Tibet and illegally annexed it in 1959.

I believe that it is not sufficient just to protest against the massive violations of human rights that are taking place in Tibet. It is also necessary to state clearly that Tibet was not a part of China before the invasion occurred, that China violated international law by invading Tibet, and that it continues to violate international law by denying the Tibetan people their right to self-determination.

Most of all, I think we need to take a realistic look at China's global strategy. In doing so, we need to heed the words of Liu Xiaobo, the Chinese dissident who was not allowed to attend the ceremony in Oslo when he was awarded the Nobel Peace Prize in 2010 and who died in prison last July. More than a decade ago, Liu warned that if China continued to rise as a dictatorship, the result will not only be another catastrophe for the Chinese people but likely also a disaster for the spread of liberal democracy in the world. We need to remember Liu Xiaobo, study his writings about the relationship between international security and political freedom, and shape a policy toward China that recognizes the dangers we face and is consistent with the values we cherish.

We also need to remember that the struggle for Tibetan rights cannot be separated from the fight for human rights and freedom in China.

In 2008, following the outbreak of violence in Lhasa, Liu and 28 other Chinese dissidents appealed to Chinese leaders to engage in direct dialogue with the Dalai Lama and expressed their hope that the Chinese and Tibetan people will do away with the misunderstandings between them, develop their interactions with each other, and achieve unity. That is the path to a more democratic China and to a more peaceful world. Thank you, Mr. Chairman.

[The prepared statement of Mr. Gershman follows:]

<u>Chinese Expansionism and the Future of Tibet</u>

Testimony by Carl Gershman, President of the National Endowment for Democracy

At the Hearing of the Subcommittee on Asia and the Pacific of the Committee on Foreign Affairs

On "U.S. Policy Towards Tibet: Access, Religious Freedom, and Human Rights"

December 6, 2017

Thank you, Chairman Yoho and Ranking Member Sherman, for the invitation to testify before the Subcommittee on this important matter. I want to begin by noting an article that appeared last week in *The Washington Post* by David Ignatius that was provocatively entitled "China's Plan to Rule the World." The article referenced several reports commissioned by the Pentagon and the Air Force, one of which describes China's economic and military buildup as "perhaps the most ambitious grand strategy undertaken by a single nation-state in modern times." The article described several dimensions of the strategy, in particular the $1 trillion "One Belt, One Road" trade and infrastructure plan that dwarfs by some seven times the Marshall Plan in postwar Europe, and that has "the strategic intent of constructing a Chinese-led regional order in Eurasia."

While the article alluded to China's military buildup in Asia, which has alarmed Japan, India, and other countries in the region, it actually understated the scope of China's growing power projection by overlooking its far-reaching efforts in the fields media, education, and political values and ideas. This is sometimes called soft-power, but a study of rising authoritarian influence, that was released just hours ago by the National Endowment for Democracy, says that it is more properly called "sharp power" since its goal is to pierce and penetrate targeted populations by manipulating and distorting the information that reaches them. China spends an estimated $10-15 billion on such sharp-power efforts.

The United States and many other countries have tended to take a benign view of China's policies because Xi Jinping tries to present himself to the world as a global citizen, and he does not indulge in the brazen behavior of Russia's Vladimir Putin. In addition, the illusion still persists that the integration of China into the global economy and political order will moderate its behavior and encourage its internal liberalization. In fact, the threat posed by China to the world order has increased with its growing economic power, and repression is worse today than at any time since the death of Mao Zedong four decades ago.

Nowhere is this repression more cruel than in Tibet, where the Chinese government is pursuing a policy that the Dalai Lama has called "cultural genocide." In addition to the systematic effort to destroy the Tibetan religion, language, culture, and distinct national identity, China has flooded Tibet with Han Chinese settlers, placed monasteries under direct government control, arrested and tortured writers, and forcibly resettled more than two million nomads in urban areas, destroying their traditional way of life and disrupting the fragile ecosystem of the Tibet Plateau. The death and likely murder in prison in July 2015 of Tenzin Delek Rinpoche, the beloved community leader and spiritual teacher, is emblematic of this oppression, which has led to the self-immolation - in desperate protest - of more than 150 Tibetans.

The continued Tibetan resistance to Chinese oppression exposes the falseness of China's claim to the legitimacy of its rule in Tibet, which rests on the assertion, stated in a White Paper issued by the

Chinese government in 2015, that "Tibet has been an integral part of China since antiquity." China insists that it won't resume the negotiations over Tibet's status that it broke off in 2010 until the Dalai Lama agrees to this assertion, something he cannot do since it is contradicted by the historical literature and overlooks the fact that Communist China invaded Tibet and illegally annexed it in 1959.

I believe that it is not sufficient just to protest against the massive violations of human rights that are taking place in Tibet. It is also necessary to state clearly that Tibet was not a part of China before the invasion occurred, that China violated international law by invading Tibet, and that it continues to violate international law by denying the Tibetan people their right to self-determination.

Most of all, I think we need to take a realistic look at China's global strategy. In doing so, we should heed the words of Liu Xiaobo, the Chinese dissident who was not allowed to attend the ceremony in Oslo when he was awarded the Nobel Peace Prize in 2010, and who died in prison last July. More than a decade ago, Liu warned that if China continued to rise as a dictatorship, "the results will not only be another catastrophe for the Chinese people but likely also a disaster for the spread of liberal democracy in the world."

We need to remember Liu Xiaobo, study his writings about the relationship between international security and political freedom, and shape a policy toward China that recognizes the dangers we face and is consistent with the values we cherish.

We also need to remember that the struggle for Tibetan rights cannot be separated from the fight for human rights and freedom in China. In 2008, following the outbreak of violence in Lhasa, Liu and 28 other Chinese dissidents appealed to China's leaders to engage in direct dialogue with the Dalai Lama, and expressed their "hope that the Chinese and Tibetan people will do away with the misunderstandings between them, develop their interactions with each other, and achieve unity." That is the path to a more democratic China and a more peaceful world.

Mr. YOHO. Thank you. I appreciate it.

I have just been informed that they are going to call votes between 4 and 4:15, and so if we can adhere to the 5 minutes. What I want to read out here is Freedom House's latest freedom index ranked Tibet second least free place on the planet, slightly better than Syria but less free than North Korea. I don't know how that can happen. Yet the situation in Syria and North Korea get far more media coverage, thanks to the crisis and the threats of terrorism and nuclear war. Tibetan leaders lament that their nonviolent movement is ignored while violent movements and violent regimes succeed. Tibetans are nationalists, but they are not seeking ethnic purity in Tibet like the militant Buddhist nationalists in Burma, nor are the Tibetans seeking their own state like the Kurds in Iraq. Instead, the Tibetan leadership is pursuing a middle way approach that seeks limited autonomy within China. They just want to be left alone.

And as I said, Mr. Gere, I am going to stop there and let you finish up your talk and your recommendations.

Mr. GERE. Yes. We have recommendations. Sorry. Look, we think that the Policy Act—the passing of bipartisan bill H.R. 1872, the Reciprocal Access to Tibet Act of 2017, is important. It is a win. It is international norms, the rule of law, which is something that is very hard to find inside of Tibet and also China. But there are norms.

If they want to be the super power that they claim to be and the world leader they claim to be, these norms are to be followed, and that is part of what the Tibet Policy Act is aiming towards, but this is very specific in terms of that reciprocal access to Tibet.

The Senate version of that, H. Con. Resolution 89, the same. These things need to be passed, and they can be passed, and I think it is important.

I think another important part of the Tibet Policy Act was to encourage the negotiations between the Dalai Lama's representatives and the Chinese Government. We have not done that recently, and this needs to be the forefront of what our policy is with China. It is not unreasonable, and it is actually good for China. To resolve these Tibetan issues is good for everyone, especially the Chinese.

It is funny, every time there is a new President of the People's Republic of China, I somehow get a message to them and say: The first thing that you can do is become Time's Man of the Year by coming to a conclusion with this Tibetan problem. A picture of Xi Jinping with the Dalai Lama shaking hands and coming to a conclusion costs the Chinese nothing. The Tibetan point of view is one of nonviolence and inclusion.

I think another point, and I have been making this for years, is that the administration can't do this alone. The U.S. can't do it alone. We have to work with our European counterparts, and not just in Europe but in other countries as well, in a multilateral approach. And I think, unfortunately, we don't have a State Department that is fully manned at this point, but this is the kind of thing the State Department should be spending time and energy with, counterparts in our allied countries around the world.

The Chinese are very good at making separate deals with every country. If we were a unified world in confronting these problems in China, we really could get somewhere.

The U.S. Special Coordinator for Tibetan Issues is extremely important. We have yet to have one. This has never happened. Greg Craig was the very first one—when was it, what was the year, 1991? Nineteen ninety-seven was the first time, and we have had—we have been fully employed in that job since then. We have gone a year now without having a Special Coordinator for Tibetan Issues, which is part of the Tibet Policy Act. I think it is reasonable to expect Congress to demand that that position be filled with a quality high-level person, as it has always been.

I think the access issue is very important. I think His Holiness meeting with either the President of the United States or Secretary Rex Tillerson I think is also important. I think a man-to-man meeting and understanding of the issues, of understanding where the Tibetan people are coming from, not how they are characterized by the Communist Party, but to hear it from the Tibetans themselves, no better representative than His Holiness the Dalai Lama.

I think we have to continue our humanitarian assistance to the Tibetan communities. It is not that much money, frankly. And the millions of dollars is doing extraordinary things. We have to continue that. We can't allow that to be taken away.

Another thing we have talked about for some time is establishing a consulate in Lhasa. Completely doable, and, again, part of the modern world. If people are traveling—the Chinese are traveling here; Americans want to and should be traveling to Tibet—and we should have a consulate. And I think, beyond that, we should say to the Chinese: If you want a consulate in Atlanta, I think you can give us one in Lhasa.

Mr. YOHO. That is right. I am going to have to cut you off and go on to Mr. Sherman, but what I would like you to do is go ahead and submit those so we can put them in the record and we can review those because I think they are very valid points.

Mr. GERE. Thank you, Mr. Chairman.

Mr. YOHO. I really appreciate it.

We will go to the ranking member, Mr. Brad Sherman, of California.

Mr. SHERMAN. We have got to get the truth out. I want to talk a little bit about the Voice of America in getting truthful information to the people of Tibet. We also need to get the truth out to the American people, and as I commented in my opening statement, China has a system of restricting the number of movies that it will accept from the United States so they can—they have got each studio in their quotas. They can then intimidate American studios not to cover Tibet. They can even intimidate American studios not to feature actors that are concerned with Tibet.

Mr. Gere, I would like to see you in more movies. What is China doing and how do they use this quota system not only to affect you but to terrorize everyone else in the entertainment business in the United States into not being the second Richard Gere and the third Richard Gere on this issue?

Mr. GERE. Well, I think it is a little more complicated than you are presenting it. There definitely is a quota, and the quota is controlled by the Communist Party for sure, but it is in partnership with the exhibitors in China.

Now, if there is a quota, obviously, the exhibitors are going to want movies that are going to make the most money. So they end up being, you know, CGI blockbuster movies.

Mr. SHERMAN. If there was a movie that everyone in the world was talking about and it was made by a studio that they had on their blacklist, they might still let it in?

Mr. GERE. No, highly unlikely. That is not true——

Mr. SHERMAN. Even then, they might not let it in?

Mr. GERE.—if it is blacklisted.

But the power is this, is that they can say the villain is no longer going to be Chinese, and Richard Gere is not going to play the hero. They can say that.

Mr. SHERMAN. So you are saying the Chinese would be fine as long as you played the villain?

Mr. GERE. They might. They might.

Mr. SHERMAN. Right.

Mr. GERE. They might. But clearly this is control of the——

Mr. SHERMAN. Not only their ability to control one movie, but they can turn to a studio that has 10 blockbusters and say: Well, maybe we will let one of them in, or maybe we will let eight of them in. There are some other good movies for some other studios just down the street. Maybe we will let one of them in, and maybe we will let seven in. Do we like your studio? Will we give one studio seven movies because they don't have Richard Gere in any of their films?

Mr. GERE. Look, I am sure that is part of it, but I think, again, it is more complex than that. I think the more sinister part of this—and it is not only in movies; it is in everything with the Chinese—people self-edit before the Chinese even have to say anything; they are so terrified of the Chinese.

Mr. SHERMAN. Right.

Mr. GERE. And a lot of this in terms of the movies is the Chinese don't have to say, "Don't have Richard Gere," whoever; the studios themselves will self-edit that way.

Now, personally, to me, it doesn't matter. I don't make those kinds of movies anyhow. I make very small, dramatic films. So it has had no impact on my career, zero. But it is a complicated situation. The root of it is the fear of the Communist Party ruling out your product getting into China.

Mr. SHERMAN. But there might be a Hollywood actor, big name, that does make a career in those big budget movies, and if that person was sitting next to you today, I am not sure that it would be lost on the studio that they have to maintain a good relationship with China.

I want to move on to the issue of the Voice of America and Radio Free Asia. The Chinese are jamming many of these signals. That proves to me that they are of some importance. How important are they to the Tibetan people, and what additional steps can we take, Mr. Tethong?

Mr. TETHONG. The Voice of America and Radio Free Asia broadcasts are a lifeline to the Tibetan people. If it were not for these broadcasts, the Tibetan people would be completely starved of any real and correct information of what is happening in their own backyard, as well as in the rest of the world.

We have been relatively successful in getting information out of Tibet, as I stated earlier, but there is a lot more we can do. We need to find more people who are able to communicate inside Tibet and to bring the information out. So that requires, I think, more resources, to say the least.

Mr. SHERMAN. I want to get one more question in. China seems to be demolishing religious sites and restricting religious practice in Tibet. What can—I will ask both Mr. Gere and Mr. Gershman— what can the United States do to push China to promote the rebuilding of destroyed Tibetan Buddhist monasteries and holy sites?

Mr. GERSHMAN. Thank you, Mr. Chairman. As I suggested in my remarks, I think it is important to raise the ante in the way we deal with China on this issue. It is important that we raise these issues, that we protest these issues, but I think we also need more leverage in the relationship.

And I believe we will get more leverage in the relationship if we raise what is the fundamental issue, which is that China's rule, its occupation, its control of Tibet is illegitimate.

Tibet was an independent entity, if not an independent country, when China invaded in 1949 and 1950 and when it annexed Tibet in 1959. This is the issue China itself has raised in saying that it won't talk to the Dalai Lama until he says China was part of— Tibet was part of China since antiquity.

Mr. SHERMAN. Which is just false.

Mr. GERSHMAN. Of course. But I think it is very, very important. And it can start with the Congress, if it is not going to start with the administration, to raise this point repeatedly to put this issue on the agenda. And once you have done that, in my view, you will get China's attention on the kind of issues you are raising.

I just want to say one other point about information, which you have raised so well. The National Endowment for Democracy just today, a few hours ago, issued a report on what was called sharp power, which is China's information plan, information system, to control, distort, manipulate, the information that reaches the publics in the West and Russia as well. But it is part of the rising authoritarian influence in the world.

It also is very important in our universities with these Confucius Institutes. There are over 100 in our society. They control academic freedom. They control how China is taught in the universities. And they also exist in countries all over the world—because the report focuses just on four countries—it could focus on many more—Poland, Slovakia, Argentina, and Peru. But it is all over the world today where they are expanding their influence in the field of information. We don't call it soft power. We call it sharp power because the goal is to perforate, to penetrate the way a syringe does, democratic societies.

Mr. YOHO. Thank you. I appreciate you. And you have brought that out very well. And we are going to come back to that.

And we will next go to Mr. Scott Perry.

Mr. PERRY. Thanks, Mr. Chairman.

Thanks, gentlemen, for your attendance today. I will tell you that I remain very frustrated with the pace of things in Tibet. And while I listened to the dialogue here today, Mr. Gere, I couldn't agree with you more. The consulate in Lhasa, it should be like the minimum standard, right? It shouldn't even be a question for us. The Special Coordinator for Tibetan Issues, I agree completely.

But I got to tell you: Communists are Communists. And they have been Communists as long as—that is what they are, and they do what they do. Tibet is a horrifically strangled area of the world, and it has been ever since I have been. In my memory, that is all Tibet has been, which is an example of the oppression of communism. And as we sit here today, their culture is slowly but steadily being strangled away from them as they participate in it literally, right? When you talk about the movies, that they self-correct, that is their own participation and their own demise. And so, while we talk about the things that we are today, it seems to me that there needs to be a new view of this, new actions taken. The actions we have taken, asking for a special coordinator and asking for more dialogue, that is not getting the job done, is the point. It is not doing—the Chinese are playing long ball. They look at things in terms of hundreds of years. We can't get past dinner tonight.

So my question to you is: I wonder—and maybe because you are all obviously very involved in Tibet and what Tibet would do, and so maybe these questions are ill-founded for you, but I just wonder what your perception would be if the United States—what would China do if the United States recognized the Tibetan Government in exile? Anybody?

Mr. GERSHMAN. We would get their attention.

Mr. GERE. Yeah. Yeah. Basically, that is it. You would get their attention.

Look, the Chinese—and it has been funny. We have been, for many decades, you know, we have been talking about this and with really smart Representatives and Senators, people in government, State Department, and everyone knows how the Chinese function. It is nibbling. They nibble at the edges of the world.

Mr. PERRY. Consistently.

Mr. GERE. Consistently. And we back off. And every time we back off a step, they take that step in every area, whether it is land, whether it is law, whether it is morals, ethics, whatever it may be. If we back off, they take it. And we have to say no. We have to recognize it for what it is, say it for what it is, call it for what it is, and just tell the truth straightforward.

Now, obviously, it is difficult financially for us; economically it could be. But this is why I say we have to do it with the rest of the world. The EU has to be a partner in this with us. And we have to put the energy and time it takes to create that partnership. Then we have real teeth dealing with the Chinese.

Mr. PERRY. I would agree with you. And I think that that this needs to be—if we believe in freedom, and autonomous rule, and especially for the people of Tibet, who don't get any credit for trying to be——

Mr. GERE. For nonviolence.

Mr. PERRY. For their nonviolence, right? Who would be a better partner with the United States of America than the people of Tibet and the government?

Mr. GERE. Also for China. Who would be a partner for them than the real Tibetans? Not the ones they pretend to——

Mr. PERRY. Well, they have a different view of things. They are not interested in a good partner. They are interested in control of everything around them, including Tibet. But——

Mr. GERE. Including their own people.

Mr. PERRY. Absolutely. Which they intend to make Tibet, of course.

So I would imagine it could—it could just be unilateral action by this President. And while I imagine many people find fault with the President, he could tell the President of China that we are not going to have any more substantive discussions until you drop your demand that the Dalai Lama recognize that Tibet is a Chinese territory, right? He could start with that.

Mr. GERE. Great. Great.

Mr. GERSHMAN. Absolutely.

Mr. PERRY. Unilaterally. It doesn't take an act of Congress. And he might actually get some good press for 5 minutes in a day, right? He might actually get some good press for that. But it seems to me that this Congress—and we should put a package together that includes a minimum of these things that we support, even if it is just in a resolution, a consulate and these demands regarding the Chinese Government in regard to Tibet, and move that swiftly through the House and the Senate, and demand action, and demand a signature and then action on it.

Mr. GERE. God bless you. That is terrific. Thank you.

Mr. GERSHMAN. And it was China—I just want to note. It is China that is raising the issue of history.

Mr. PERRY. Well, of course, it is. Like Mr. Gere said, when we—when good people are silent, that is when tyranny continues on its march. And we are busy people around the world trying to do good things and trying to do good things in our own country. But we have to recognize the small things that we can do that can make a huge difference. And, to me, that is a very small ask to say to China: You are not going to revise history. We won't accept it. And there are going to be consequences to your actions.

Mr. Chairman, I appreciate your indulgence, and I yield.

Mr. YOHO. No, I appreciate you bringing that up, very important. Now we will next go to Mr. Gerry Connolly.

Mr. CONNOLLY. Thank you, Mr. Chairman.

And thank you all for being here today.

For the record, working for the Tom Lantos Commission Defending Freedoms Project, I sort of have adopted the case of Lobsang Tsering, who is now serving 10 years in Chinese prison under the trumped-up charge of inciting self-immolation. And there is some reason to believe he may have been—you know, his testimony may have been coerced. But what this is really all about is the expression of dissent. And certainly I call upon the Chinese Government to release Lobsang Tsering and everyone else who is a prisoner of conscience with respect to the subject, Tibet.

I would also say that, probably unlike most of my colleagues here, I went to Tibet in 1986. I led the first joint Senate and House staffdel to Tibet. We were the first allowed in, that I know of, by the Chinese Government. And it was a remarkable experience because what we saw was the evidence—this was 31 years ago now—of the Chinese plan to repopulate the Tibetan homeland with the Han, non-Tibetans. And there are a lot of Chinese. So not that hard to do if you can get Chinese willing to live there. We saw the destruction, both from the cultural revolution ravages and current suppression of monasteries, of places—sacred shrines and so forth, really important to Tibetan Buddhism.

We saw, certainly, and heard some low-key testimony of people who had themselves been brutalized, incarcerated, and persecuted. We saw the propaganda efforts of the Chinese Government in terms of the narrative about what Tibet was and had always been. This is 31 years ago. In Beijing, they insisted we meet with the Panchen Lama—that particular Panchen Lama is now dead. And I felt like I was meeting Quisling, you know, the Norwegian leader who basically did the bidding of the Nazi occupiers in Norway during World War II. I thought, I can't believe I am hearing this alternative view of the universe and Tibetan culture and religion from somebody with your title and your prestige. And I think—frankly, I don't think Tibetans listened to him. But it was a remarkable thing, nonetheless, in terms of how the Chinese staged this. So everything I am hearing 31 years later is still true.

Mr. Gere, you talked about nibbling away. But they are also systematic and very patient. They just don't give up. And I guess I would just ask any and all of you: So here we are, 31 years later for me. Has it gotten better? Has it gotten worse? How successful do you think the Chinese Government is in consolidating that set of policies to their end, which is basically to make Tibet Chinese, culturally, ethnically, politically?

Mr. TETHONG. As far as we know, even though the Chinese have been very successful on a superficial level, we know—we believe that the Tibetans have not given in, so to speak. In fact, the Tibetan spirit is still very strong. And I think that is what drives people to send information out——

Mr. CONNOLLY. If I can interrupt you, so what has happened demographically? What percentage of Tibet today, population wise, is ethnic Han?

Mr. TETHONG. It is difficult to get exact demographics because——

Mr. CONNOLLY. Of course.

Mr. TETHONG [continuing]. The figures are controlled. But there may be anywhere from 1 million to 6 million Chinese on the Tibetan Plateau, which before 1959, may have been less than 100,000.

Mr. CONNOLLY. That is right.

Mr. TETHONG. But most of these Chinese will come with special privileges. They have this ability to set up house right away without the house registration. They are given other incentives, through business and government, which are denied to many Tibetans right in that local area, including Tibetans from other parts of Tibet who are not allowed to move around. So, with all that incentive, there are increasing numbers of Chinese in the urban areas. But we also know that most Chinese would prefer not to be in Tibet because the high altitude is not the best place to be.

Mr. CONNOLLY. Right.

Mr. TETHONG. So that is another reality that is also unfolding at the same time.

Mr. CONNOLLY. But, still, a lot of people move there.

If I am allowed one final observation: Mr. Gershman, so like the Presidents of the last two decades, Mr. Trump has met with the Dalai Lama, right? And the United States, both in the form of the Secretary of State and the President, when they have an opportunity with President Xi or other senior Chinese officials, we brought up Tibet, and human rights in Tibet, and the situation in Tibet consistently? Have I got that right?

Mr. GERE. No, not at all.

Mr. CONNOLLY. Am I wrong?

Mr. GERE. You are wrong.

Mr. CONNOLLY. Well, Lord almighty. Help clarify, Mr. Gere.

Mr. GERE. No, His Holiness has not met with either Trump or Tillerson. And there is a question as to whether or not that will happen. I think it should happen. Of course, it should happen. It has happened since the first George Bush and in—I think it was 1991, I think, when the first meeting was. Every President since then has spent serious time with His Holiness and his representatives. But it has not happened thus far.

Mr. CONNOLLY. Well, final point——

Mr. GERE. And we don't know——

Mr. CONNOLLY. I know. Thank you, Mr. Gere.

I wanted Mr. Gershman just to talk about the political points. So are we using our diplomatic spigots to press home this case whenever we have that opportunity with senior Chinese officials?

Mr. GERSHMAN. I don't think so. I don't—the issue may occasionally get raised in a symbolic way when meetings take place. But what really I was calling for, in my brief testimony, was a comprehensive, integrated policy that recognizes the full scope of the challenge that is not just, you know, focusing on Tibet because it goes so much beyond that in China's global policy today. And its influence and power are expanding. You just have to look at the alarm in a country like India or in Japan to understand how the countries in the neighborhood are viewing this.

And I think we need to be in touch with our allies on this. And we need to shape a coordinated policy which does—should put the issue on the table and raise the issue of human rights, but as I said in my testimony, I think we have to go beyond that. And we have to look at the fundamental, underlying issue, which is that the Tibet people are being denied their right to self-determination. The Dalai Lama has not—what the Dalai Lama wants with the Middle Way policy is genuine autonomy. He is not talking about independence. He is talking about genuine autonomy. And I think we have to get behind that and support it vigorously and also then to raise the issue of the status of Tibet.

Mr. YOHO. I thank you for your time.

Mr. CONNOLLY. Mr. Chairman, thank you for your courtesy.

Mr. YOHO. Yes, sir.

We will next go to the lady from Florida, Chairman Emeritus——

Ms. ROS-LEHTINEN. Thank you very much. I am no lady; I am a Member of Congress.

And to follow up on Mr. Connolly's remarks, I wanted to ask, Mr. Connolly, when you led that staffdel, was that when you were a member of the Senate Foreign Relations Committee? Because I have heard that rumor once or twice.

Mr. CONNOLLY. So I am going to break this news to you and confirm it: I was a senior staff member on the Senate Foreign Relations Committee——

Ms. ROS-LEHTINEN. I had no idea. I have never heard that.

Mr. CONNOLLY. Yeah. Yeah.

Ms. ROS-LEHTINEN. Thank you so much. Mr.

CONNOLLY. You are more than welcome.

Ms. ROS-LEHTINEN. Well, Mr. Gere, you had—that is a private joke we have going.

You had recommended in your testimony that the United States "urge the new Chinese leadership to reevaluate the stability maintenance approach applied in Tibet and the dominance of the security apparatus."

I would like to ask you for your thoughts on whether this stability maintenance approach is having the positive impact on stability that it claims.

Mr. GERE. Well, stability maintenance is the hard fist. That is basically what it is. There are no carrots associated with this at all. It is just blind and complete repression. There is no incentive for the Tibetans. It is an approach that is doomed to failure. And the only way that it could succeed is if they actually kill all the Tibetans. And they have created such a pressure cooker situation that, of course, there is a point where people feel that they have nothing to lose. And then you see these self-immolations.

Now, there is very little violence against Chinese. It hasn't exploded that way. This is not a terrorist community. And the limited ability for Tibetans to express their pain and their suffering is releasing now in the self-immolations. I mean, it is one of the saddest things one could ever imagine. Monks and nuns and laypeople who, out of despair and love and compassion for their own people, their own culture, this is the only cry that they can make that can possibly be heard. The tools of expression are not given to them. They have been taken away in the extreme. So this is a policy that is doomed to failure on all levels unless it is complete genocide.

Ms. ROS-LEHTINEN. Horrific.

And we have heard report after report today, Mr. Chairman, about the invasive, the restrictive, the brutal nature of the Chinese security apparatus as it attempts to erase the culture and the identity of the Tibetan people, demolishing Buddhist sites, attacking the language of Tibet.

Do you think that this approach is undermining the very stability that it is attempting to institute?

Mr. GERE. Well, look, we have been positing—and I think rationally, not just emotionally—the solution to the problem is the Dalai Lama. The solution is someone who is deeply respected and honored by the Tibetan people, who is an honest broker. If they sat down with him and said: Well, what is really meaningful to you? The reality is it is something they can freely give away. It is the free expression of their culture, their religion, their concern for each other as a community of like feelings and emotions and vision of possibility of the future. There is nothing negative in the Tibetan soul that would hurt the Chinese experiment.

It is a fool's errand that the Chinese are on here that ultimately hurts them as well. This is a huge problem for them, Tibet. You think they want to have this hearing in the U.S. Congress and the kind of outrage that is expressing itself around the world of the treatment of Tibetans? It is no good for anyone. So it is a radical rethinking of this.

But I also want to come back to what Carl was saying. Tibet is not an isolated situation. To deal with the Tibetan situation, you have got to see all of Asia. And you have to see the 100-year, the 200-year plan of China and how they will take over Siberia. They will take over the Turkestan areas. They will take over Southern Europe. There is no question about this.

Ms. ROS-LEHTINEN. The long-haul game that Mr. Perry——

Mr. GERE. They are moving in that direction. And they are moving at a quicker pace than even they realized they could.

Ms. ROS-LEHTINEN. Thank you so much.

Mr. Chairman, thanks for letting me be a part of this subcommittee today. Thank you, sir.

Mr. YOHO. I always enjoy having your input and your wisdom. And I appreciate it.

I want to go back to something. You know, and I think, Mr. Gershman, you have all brought it up. And that is the aggression of China. And I think you are spot on. And we have said this before, that they are going to fail. China will fail at this because they fear freedom and liberties. But that is a universal belief all people have. They want to be free. They want to be self-determining. They want to be self-governing. And we are so fortunate in this country to have a system that allows that. And we need to sometimes take a pause and look at that and really embrace the freedoms we have in this country because it doesn't take you long to go to another country to see what is happening, the encroachment on freedoms. I mean, the guy in North Korea that was trying to get out, they shoot people trying to get out of their country, and we have got people wanting to come into our country. It is backwards. And China will continue to fail until they embrace their people and empower them. Yeah, they are doing great right now. But it is not long term.

With the 19th Communist Party Congress that was in China where Xi Jinping consolidated his power—and this is almost a rhetorical question—how do you believe Xi Jinping's elevation will affect Tibet, for the better or for the worse?

Mr. GERE. There is nothing to indicate that he is a good guy, okay?

Mr. YOHO. Mr. Tethong?

Mr. TETHONG. From what we have seen in the last 5 years of his tenure, first, things have gotten worse in Tibetan areas and restrictions have increased. And the deliberate attempt to diminish Tibetan culture and identity is very apparent. So I think it is difficult to see anything promising in the near future.

Mr. YOHO. You are right. And the same thing is going on in Taiwan and in Hong Kong. And they are influencing—I mean, even

South Korea. The effect China has on Australia now is mind boggling.

Mr. Gershman, do you have anything you want to add to that?

Mr. GERSHMAN. Well, you are absolutely right, Mr. Chairman. I think what we are seeing today around Asia, including Australia, yes, is alarm at what they see as a retreating West and an expanding China, an expanding influence of China.

I just want to mention one thing in response to Congresswoman Ros-Lehtinen's point about the failure of the Chinese policy. I quoted in my testimony the 29 Chinese dissidents who were calling for dialogue with the Dalai Lama, one of whom, the lead one, was Liu Xiaobo. And they said that a country that wishes to avoid partition of its territory must first avoid divisions among its nationalities. And they call for eliminating animosity that brings about—to bring about national reconciliation.

The more they oppress the Tibetan people, the greater the likelihood is that there will be less willingness to try to reach some kind of a compromise, more readiness to resist. And that is what we are seeing today. It is a desperate form of resistance today. But, you know, as you suggest, Mr. Chairman, authoritarian rule is never secure. And I think that we have to have patience.

The Chinese have patience. We have to not only have patience and embrace freedom. We have to recognize that we do have rivals. Those rivals have plans. And we have to develop strategies to try to deal with the threats that we face in a realistic and comprehensive way, building alliances, as Richard says, because I think there are a lot of countries that are looking to us now to support in leadership on this and are very, very concerned with the international environment today.

Mr. YOHO. Thank you for your comments.

Mr. Scott Perry, you got a second round of questions?

Mr. Sherman wanted to hold off for a minute.

Mr. PERRY. Well, then I will indulge him.

The struggle over the next Dalai Lama. Just like Hong Kong, we fully expect the Chinese to influence that to the maximum that they can, and I wonder two things. What will the Tibetan people do when they see the overt interference and a puppet—is there such thing as a puppet Dalai Lama, so to speak? But I mean, as horrific and—just as horrific as that sounds, I am sure that the Chinese Government doesn't care. What would the people of Tibet do? And what should the United States be doing in advance of that expectation to ensure that the Chinese either decide that is not in their best interest or to dissuade them as much as possible?

Mr. TETHONG. Well, I think if the Chinese recognize a so-called puppet Dalai Lama, it is very likely that no Tibetan would really recognize him as the Dalai Lama. The last Panchen Lama which the Chinese recognized, he may be a decent young man, but he is finding very little open acceptance in Tibet itself. And his appearances, both among Tibetans and in China, is also very limited. I think the Chinese Government realizes that. So I don't think it will be a successful effort if they do that.

As far as what we can do from there, I think making it very clear that it is absolutely ridiculous for a Communist Party institution to recognize Tibetan Buddhist institution. I think just pointing out how ridiculous that I think is the first step in trying to prevent the Chinese from doing that.

Mr. PERRY. But without the kind of the specter of the immediacy of the issue, so to speak, is anybody going to listen to that message? I hate to say it that way. But I just don't know that anybody is going to hear that without the urgency as opposed to after the current Dalai Lama passes.

Mr. GERE. I think absolutely the U.S. Government should say it is up to the Tibetan people to make this decision. It was a laughable moment that—you know, His Holiness is an 82-year-old man. He was asked, who is going to be the next Dalai Lama? And he said, "Well, the institution is up to the Tibetan people if they want a Dalai Lama. But, beyond that, if they want the Dalai Lama, I guarantee you I will not be born in a Chinese-controlled area," at which point the Communist Party said, "It isn't up to the Dalai Lama to decide where he will be born next, it is up to the Communist Party," of course misunderstanding completely the logic process of transference of consciousness.

The U.S. Government going on record as saying that it is not up to the Communist Party, it is up to the religious authorities of the Tibetan community to make that decision, and go beyond that and say, of the free Tibetan community, religious community, to make those decisions.

Mr. PERRY. And that would be something that we could include——

Mr. GERE. Absolutely.

Mr. PERRY [continuing]. As Congress in——

Mr. GERE. And most important.

Mr. PERRY. Yeah.

Mr. GERE. Absolutely. That is terrific.

Mr. PERRY. Yeah. That would, to me, be simple, right? That would be simple.

Mr. GERE. Yes. Straightforward.

Mr. PERRY. Should the United States limit the travel of Chinese diplomats or at least raise the specter of limiting the travel of Chinese diplomats until we see any movement at all? I mean, I don't see any positive direction in this relationship between China and Tibet in my lifetime. I don't see any. So, to me, we need some game-changers here. So would that be something at least to discuss that would, at a minimum, slow down, for instance, the Chinese's— China's slow and methodical strangulation of Tibet? Would it at least have them take pause, even to just bring it up?

Mr. GERSHMAN. Well, the legislation raises the issue of reciprocation. And if journalists and U.S. officials and others are not permitted to travel to Tibet, then there should be a response to that from this country. In other words, we need a single standard. We need equality in this relationship. So I think the legislation that Congressman McGovern has drafted, as I have seen it, addresses this point well.

Mr. PERRY. Yeah. It would seem that most Americans and most people around the globe would agree that equal reciprocity is realistic and not beyond the realm of fairness, right? So——

Mr. GERSHMAN. Absolutely. And I think—on your previous point, I just want to say that it is a fundamental issue of religious freedom. And, you know, it behooves the United States.

Mr. PERRY. If not this country, who is going to stand up for that?

Mr. GERSHMAN. Everyone—I mean, in this country, we must stand up for religious freedom. And we have to get other countries to stand up for this fundamental right because what the Chinese are now doing, when the chief official of the Communist Party says that the Dalai Lama is betraying his own faith by saying that he might not reincarnate if—you know, you won't reincarnate if you cannot—if you cannot continue the work. If they are being prevented from continuing the work, it is not for the Chinese Communist Party to make that decision. They are preventing the Dalai Lama, and presumably his successor, from continuing the work of the Dalai Lama. It is up to the Dalai Lama and the Tibetan people to make that decision, not the Chinese Government. And I think we should stand up very vigorously for the principle of religious freedom.

Mr. PERRY. Thank you, Mr. Chairman, for your indulgence. I yield.

Mr. YOHO. No. I appreciate it.

Now, we will go to Mr. Sherman.

Mr. SHERMAN. The idea that the Chinese Communist Party would make a theological determination offers some comic relief to what is otherwise a very serious hearing.

Mr. GERSHMAN. I once called that shameless impudence.

Mr. SHERMAN. Mr. Gere, who is the appropriate body to identify the next Dalai Lama and to determine the existing Dalai Lama. The existing Dalai Lama has told us where he will not be reborn, but we don't know whether he will be reborn and in which, a young man or—I don't know the theology, whether it be a young man or young woman.

Mr. GERE. It could be a woman. Could be a woman. Could be—have a Western body. I mean, it is whatever——

Mr. SHERMAN. What is the group of people that will officially identify for Tibetan Buddhists who is the next Dalai Lama?

Mr. GERE. I can only give that to you generally. I can't give you the exact people. But certainly the religious community around His Holiness, the heads of the four schools of Tibetan Buddhism, certainly the heads of the Gelugpa school of Tibetan Buddhism would be intimately involved with this process.

Mr. SHERMAN. The Catholic Church has identified for the world: These are the cardinals; this is where they will meet——

Mr. GERE. It is not——

Mr. SHERMAN [continuing]. And you are saying this is more a kind of——

Mr. GERE. It is not as organized as that.

Mr. SHERMAN [continuing]. A kind of consensus of——

Mr. GERE. Well, it is quite possible, and this happened before, that this Dalai Lama will give indications of who he will be next time. And that will be part of the process.

Mr. SHERMAN. Will he identify those individuals that have the capacity to determine——

Mr. GERE. I would assume that is the case, yes.

Mr. SHERMAN. Okay. I mean, the Catholic Church makes my job easier as a non-Catholic who has to deal with religions by—this Pope will no doubt identify that these are the cardinals. And you can see how it will be easier for the United States to know who is the head of Tibetan Buddhism if the existing head of Tibetan Buddhism will tell us——

Mr. GERE. You know, these are really good questions. And, to be honest, there are things in the works now that would clarify that exact issue, that there would be a recognized body that would present to the rest of the world. The Tibetans will know. They have always known.

Mr. SHERMAN. And the heads of the major schools of Tibetan Buddhism, are they subject to Chinese pressure?

Mr. GERE. Not outside. But certainly inside, yeah.

Mr. SHERMAN. Well, I mean, I wonder, do they reside in——

Mr. GERE. No. The heads, as we know them now, are in India or Nepal.

Mr. SHERMAN. Okay.

Mr. GERE. Yeah.

Mr. SHERMAN. So, Mr. Gershman, and others. You can see how China just looks at this big piece of the map of the world and says, "We want to control that," but this is an area of the world that has been sparsely populated because it is very difficult to create food there in significant quantities. Are there particular parts of Tibet where China says, "Ah ha, that is where the gold mine is"? When they see economic development, where do they see it? What are they looking for?

Mr. GERSHMAN. I assume it is in the area of minerals. And they really are destroying the ecology of the area. And the monk I mentioned in my testimony, Tenzin Delek Rinpoche, one of the things he tried to do before he was arrested 13 years before his death in 2015 was to protect the environment because they really are destroying it and, of course, uprooting the nomads. And I think this is one really, really critical issue that we have to raise.

Obviously, there are very significant water resources in the Himalayas which are also—the Chinese would want to use for the development of energy purposes. So there are a lot of economic interests that they would have, but the fundamental interest is geopolitical. And it has led to what is now——

Mr. SHERMAN. And they are building islands in the South China Sea not because that is——

Mr. GERSHMAN. But, also, at the same time that they were doing that, there was almost, before the Party Congress, during the summer and into September, there was almost a military conflict. There was a military standoff with India over the Doklam Plateau which also involves Sikkim and Bhutan. And all of these areas are scared. And China backed off. I don't think they wanted a conflict before the Party Congress. But they are going to come back to those issues too. So they really have a very, very large geopolitical interest in maintaining that territory. And, you know, as I suggested, they invaded that territory. They occupy it illegally. And I think that has to be said.

Mr. SHERMAN. I will ask one more question, and anyone else. Is there any concern in Beijing that their access to the U.S. market for all their exports could in any way be affected by their persecution of the people of Tibet?

Mr. GERE. I mean, there is no reason for them to fear it. We have rolled over.

Mr. SHERMAN. Right.

Mr. GERE. The U.S. has rolled over. And, unfortunately——

Mr. SHERMAN. I think that answers it. And the question for us is, what do we do to change the answer to that through our policy?

I will yield back.

Mr. GERE. Well, I think what we discussed before, and Mr. Perry, I think, very cleanly described the way forward. There were half a dozen clear, simple, rational things that we can do and make part of our law. And if it is immediately making it the sense of the Congress, so be it. Move it into the territory of absolute law as the Tibet Policy Act is.

Mr. YOHO. Well, they have called votes, and we have to go. But I want to tell you how much we really appreciate this. And what we look for—I don't like to have meetings to have meetings. We like to have legislation come out of this. And we will round up the members that were here, bring some ideas together, and you should see some positive movement.

I was at a conference a couple of years ago, and we had a lot of the generals, retired generals, active generals, of the United States. And they were saying that we are going through a tectonic shift in world powers that we have not seen since pre-World War II. And now we see the rise of China with the 19th Congress and Xi Jinping came out and said that the era of China has come, that it is time for them to take the world stage. You know, I find that very threatening. And, as you have said, we have fed this monster because we demand cheap things. And it is time to change the narrative and just say: The game is over, and we are going to invest in like-minded allies. Like-minded allies believe in liberties and freedoms, those things that we talked about, the things that we hold dearly in this country. And I think you are seeing the world divide along these lines. What we know is a government that expects the people to serve a party I don't think will be long-lasting, as you brought up, whereas you have a government that serves the people is the way to go. And I think the good guys will win on this.

Mr. GERSHMAN. I want to thank you, Mr. Chairman. Your voice and the voice of your colleagues is extremely important on this issue and on the issue of freedom fundamentally. And I want to thank you.

Mr. YOHO. Well, I appreciate you all. Have a good time.

Mr. GERE. Listen, from my side, I think this is one of the best testimonies and interactions with all of you in Congress that I have ever seen. And I want to thank you from the bottom of my heart, and I think everyone else here who cares about Tibet. Thank you so much.

Mr. SHERMAN. I want to point out. She doesn't want me to mention her. But there is, of course, a Special Coordinator for Tibet. My wife served in that office for several years. She continues to work at the State Department in human rights. So I want to give her a shout out.

[Whereupon, at 4:17 p.m., the subcommittee was adjourned.]

APPENDIX

SUBCOMMITTEE HEARING NOTICE
COMMITTEE ON FOREIGN AFFAIRS
U.S. HOUSE OF REPRESENTATIVES
WASHINGTON, DC 20515-6128

Subcommittee on Asia and the Pacific
Ted Yoho (R-FL), Chairman

November 29, 2017

TO: MEMBERS OF THE COMMITTEE ON FOREIGN AFFAIRS

You are respectfully requested to attend an OPEN hearing of the Committee on Foreign Affairs, to be held by the Subcommittee on Asia and the Pacific in Room 2172 of the Rayburn House Office Building (and available live on the Committee website at http://www.ForeignAffairs.house.gov):

DATE: Wednesday, December 6, 2017

TIME: 2:00 p.m.

SUBJECT: U.S. Policy Towards Tibet: Access, Religious Freedom, and Human Rights

WITNESSES: Mr. Richard Gere
Chair of the Board of Directors
International Campaign for Tibet

Mr. Tenzin Tethong
Director of the Tibetan Service
Radio Free Asia

Mr. Carl Gershman
President
National Endowment for Democracy

By Direction of the Chairman

COMMITTEE ON FOREIGN AFFAIRS

MINUTES OF SUBCOMMITTEE ON _______*Asia and the Pacific*_______ HEARING

Day__*Wednesday*__Date__*December 6, 2017*__Room_____*2172*_____

Starting Time _____*2:37*_____ Ending Time _____*4:15*_____

Recesses [____] (____to____) (____to____) (____to____) (____to____) (____to____) (____to____)

Presiding Member(s)
Rep. Yoho

Check all of the following that apply:

Open Session ☑
Executive (closed) Session ☐
Televised ☐

Electronically Recorded (taped) ☐
Stenographic Record ☐

TITLE OF HEARING:

U.S. Policy Toward Tibet: Access, Religious Freedom, and Human Rights

SUBCOMMITTEE MEMBERS PRESENT:

Rep. Ted Yoho, Rep. Scott Perry, Rep. Steve Chabot
Rep. Brad Sherman, Rep. Tulsi Gabbard, Rep. Dina Titus, Rep. Gerald Connolly

NON-SUBCOMMITTEE MEMBERS PRESENT: *(Mark with an * if they are not members of full committee.)*

Rep. Ileana Ros-Lehtinen
*Rep. Jim McGovern**

HEARING WITNESSES: Same as meeting notice attached? Yes ☑ No ☐
(If "no", please list below and include title, agency, department, or organization.)

STATEMENTS FOR THE RECORD: *(List any statements submitted for the record.)*

Rep. Eliot Engel - SFR
Rep. Gerald Connolly - SFR
Rep. Dina Titus - QFR

TIME SCHEDULED TO RECONVENE_________
or
TIME ADJOURNED _____*4:15*_____

Subcommittee Staff Associate

FINAL

<u>Statement for the Record</u>
Ranking Member Eliot L. Engel
AP Subcommittee Hearing: "U.S. Policy Toward Tibet: Access, Religious Freedom, and
Human Rights"
December 6, 2017

Thank you, Chairman Yoho and Ranking Member Sherman. I am grateful to the both of you for
calling this hearing and bringing Congress' attention to the people of Tibet. Let me thank the
witnesses for their time, expertise and advocacy on this issue. It has been some time since the
Foreign Affairs Committee has taken up this topic in a dedicated hearing, so I appreciate the
opportunity to hear from you today. I'd also like to recognize the Lantos Human Rights
Commission led by my good friends Rep. McGovern of Massachusetts and Mr. Hultgren of
Illinois for their great work on this issue—including a Commission hearing earlier this year.

I've had the privilege to meet His Holiness, the Dalai Llama, several times including on a recent
congressional delegation trip with Leader Pelosi to Dharamshala last year. His Holiness is truly a
remarkable man. A gentle spirit, driven for within by an incredible strength and courage and
when you meet him, no matter your faith or background, you cannot help but feel the bond of
common humanity. There is no single person who has done more to advance the Tibetan cause
around the world than the Dalai Llama. As the spiritual and cultural leader of the Tibetan people,
his Holiness has done it through promoting peace, respect, tolerance and non-violence. He is
rightly revered and respected by people of all faiths—and you cannot help but be drawn into his
cause and the cause of the Tibetan people. Indeed, many in Congress have supported the plight
of Tibet.

We passed the Tibetan Policy Act of 2002 which makes it a matter of U.S. Policy to support the
aspirations of the Tibetan people to safeguard their distinct identity. We provide support for
Tibetan refugees, promote scholarships for Tibetan students, promote activities to expand
economic opportunity and environmental conservation, and Congress established a senior
coordinator for Tibetan issues at the State Department. Sadly, this is one of many, many senior
positions in the State Department that is still vacant thanks to Secretary Tillerson and our
President, Donald Trump.

In recent years, we have urged the Government of China to resume talks with the Tibetan envoys
as an essential step in reducing tensions and addressing the grievances of the Tibetan people. The
Chinese continue to have outrageous preconditions for the resumption of these dialogues, and
they have been stalled since 2010. At every turn, China's authorities have decided to pursue
policies that are counterproductive not only to human rights of Tibetans, but to China's interests
as well. By actively seeking to stamp out the Tibetan culture, language and identify through
systematic oppression, control and marginalization of the people of Tibet, Chinese authorities
raise tensions and increase the risk of unrest.

As the current Dalai Llama advances in age, although he is in good health, he has raised the issue
of his succession. Outrageously, the Chinese government has seen fit to stipulate its terms on this
issue as well, attempting to dictate **where and how** the current Dalai Llama may reincarnate—a
notion that contravenes the most basic and universally recognized right of religious freedom.

FINAL

Beijing has no role to play here: this decision on succession belongs solely to the current Dalai Llama, Tibetan Buddhist leaders, and the Tibetan people. But in doing so, China is setting the stage for conflict and controversy.

This issue—which I hope our witnesses can speak to today—should be among our top priorities in terms of the U.S. engagement with China on Tibet, but so far it hasn't received the focus it deserves.

Thank you, Mr. Chairman. I am grateful to the subcommittee for addressing the issue of the Tibetan people. I am grateful to our panelists, and I yield back.

# # #

<u>Statement for the Record</u>
Rep. Gerald Connolly
AP Subcommittee Hearing: "U.S. Policy Toward Tibet: Access, Religious Freedom, and Human Rights"
December 6, 2017

Promoting substantive dialogue between the Dalai Lama and Chinese government has been longstanding bipartisan U.S. policy for decades. According to the State Department's 2016 Report on Tibet Negotiations, "resumption of dialogue and steps to redress Tibetan grievances are critical to reducing the continuing high tensions between Tibetan and Chinese authorities." Despite this consistent policy of successive U.S. administrations, the Trump Administration has not yet reaffirmed this approach. Moreover, President Trump has declined to raise Tibet as an issue in his meetings with Chinese President Xi Jinping, proposed the elimination of funding for Tibet in his FY 2018 budget, and failed to nominate a Special Coordinator for Tibetan Issues at the State Department.

Tenuous international support for Tibet coupled with China's growing oppression of Tibetans and questions about the Dalai Lama's succession have fueled uncertainty about the future of the Tibetan resistance movement. China has recently strengthened its persecution of Tibetans through expulsions and demolitions of religious sites, the marginalization of Tibetan culture and language, and further restrictions on Tibetans' travel. The 82-year-old Dalai Lama has visited locations where his reincarnation may occur, could designate a successor before his death, or could decline to be reincarnated, ending the institution of the Dalai Lama.

At this crossroads of Tibet's future, the Dalai Lama and the Tibetan government-in-exile convened a first-of-its-kind conference, in Dharamsala, India, this past October. The Five-Fifty Forum sought to create a five-year plan for negotiations with China or chart another 50 years of resistance to Chinese control if dialogue falters. During his remarks to the conference of Tibet supporters, the Dalai Lama expressed concern regarding President Trump's "America first" policy and the use of military force rather than diplomacy to solve international problems. The Tibetan leader also praised the United States for its historic support of Tibet and human rights, particularly in Congress, and shared hope that it would continue.

Notwithstanding the Trump Administration's reluctance to engage on Tibet, the U.S. Congress has long provided and continues to uphold a strong affinity for Tibet and the Dalai Lama. The Tibetan Policy Act (TPA) of 2002 (P.L. 107-228) directs the executive branch to encourage the PRC government to dialogue with the Dalai Lama, call for the release of Tibetan political and religious prisoners, reinforce development objectives in Tibet, and support the aspirations of the Tibetan people to safeguard their distinct identity. In the 115th Congress, I have been proud to cosponsor the Reciprocal Access to Tibet Act (H.R. 1872) and H. Con. Res. 89, which both reaffirm U.S. policy toward Tibet. In June, I joined a letter to President Trump urging him to appoint the position of Special Coordinator for Tibetan Issues at the State Department as soon as possible.

Through the Tom Lantos' Commission's Defending Freedoms Project, I am an advocate for Lobsang Tsering, a former Tibetan Buddhist monk. In 2012, Chinese police detained Tsering and accused him of inciting the self-immolation of eight Tibetans, even though five of the self-immolations never occurred. It is clear to the world that such self-immolations are a last-ditch effort of desperate Tibetans living in an oppressive country with no other recourse for protest. Chinese authorities likely coerced a confession of "inciting" murder from Tsering, the implication being that the self-immolations were not protests but homicides. Tsering was convicted and sentenced to ten years in prison after a show trial where he was unrepresented by a lawyer.

Human Rights Watch correctly noted that "these prosecutions are utterly without credibility. The Chinese government seems to think it can stop self-immolation by punishing anyone who talks about it." Tsering's conviction marks the first sentence imposed against an individual for allegedly "coercing" Tibetans to self-immolate. I call on the Chinese government to release Tsering, to end the practice of imprisoning innocent Tibetans as a form of collective punishment for protests, and to stop prosecuting Tibetans for honestly discussing their plight with others, whether inside or outside of China.

Supporting Tibet in its peaceful quest for freedom for Tibetans within the confines of the Chinese constitution has been longstanding U.S. policy and remains in our national interest. The Trump Administration would do well to recognize Tibet's important role by encouraging dialogue between the Dalai Lama and the Chinese government, as the TPA requires. I look forward to hearing from our witnesses on how Congress can sustain and build upon its support for Tibet as we enter the next phase of the Tibetan resistance movement.

<u>**Questions for the Record**</u>
Rep. Dina Titus
AP Subcommittee Hearing: "U.S. Policy Towards Tibet: Access, Religious Freedom, and Human
Rights"
December 6, 2017

1. Here in the House I serve as Co-Chair of the Travel and Tourism Caucus. I know the
importance of travel and tourism to diplomacy, building relationships with other countries,
creating greater understanding of different cultures, and the economic development of a
region. Tibetans have an increasingly difficult time traveling freely due to denials of
passports by the Chinese government and lengthy application processes.

   Mr. Gere, can you discuss how increased travel opportunities, both for Tibetans and access to
   Tibet for people other than the Chinese, could benefit the people of Tibet?

   The Reciprocal Access to Tibet Act focuses on American travel to Tibetan areas, but are
   there also actions the U.S. can take to increase access to travel for Tibetans?

   Mr. Gere: As you are well-aware, the role of travel and tourism can bring tremendous benefit to
   a community but also as you know, if travel and tourism are not developed in line with the
   freewill and traditions of the local community, culture and environment can suffer a great risk of
   degradation. The person-to-person exchange is also an invaluable tool for positive growth
   and development as long as the local community is included and allowed to participate in that
   exchange. I would highly recommend a report that we at the ICT (International Campaign for
   Tibet) published in 2015 entitled *"A Policy Alienating Tibetans: the Denial of Passports to
   Tibetans as China Intensifies Control"* which will provide greater detail but in short, the
   discriminatory denial of passports for Tibetans by the Chinese Government is in contravention of
   China's own laws and international law. This is in direct contrast to an increasing number of
   Chinese citizens being granted passports who enjoy freedom of travel within their country and
   throughout the world.

   •

   The difficulty for a Tibetan person trying to obtain a passport must be seen in the context of
   tighter restrictions on movement in Tibetan areas. As a result, there are serious implications for
   the survival of Tibetan Buddhist teachings as well as the enjoyment of equal rights by Tibetans in
   the PRC.

   The transfer of Buddhist philosophical knowledge by qualified masters to the disciples is an
   integral part of the Tibetan religious practice and culture. In Tibet today, there are not many
   qualified teachers and so monks and nuns must travel to other monasteries in Tibet or outside of
   Tibet to receive teachings. A majority of traditional Tibetan Buddhist masters reside outside of
   Tibet, having fled the Chinese takeover of Tibet. The Tibetan people also view the Dalai Lama as
   the most qualified of their teachers, often wanting to receive teachings from him however, the
   denial of passports deprive them of this increasingly rare and precious opportunity.

   Last, Tibetans, like Chinese, seek the best educational opportunities. Many Tibetan parents take
   great risk to smuggle their children to India, where they are assured a holistic education they can't

get in Tibet. There are also Tibetans who have finished high school in China and would like to travel abroad to continue their studies, which obviously includes Tibetan and Buddhist studies programs. Many are denied that opportunity. The report I referred to earlier in fact quotes one such student who said, "I am a Tibetan student going to study abroad, I have worked very hard for the last two years to gain this opportunity to pass the examination. Since then I have been working hard again to apply for a passport, and have been many times to the local government, but it has refused each time, which really infuriates people."

The United States can prevail upon the Chinese Government to:

1. Abolish all discriminatory practices against Tibetans that are perceived to be root causes of Tibetan discontent and grievances, such as the unlawful denial of passports.

2. Allow foreign travel for Tibetans; issue passports to Tibetan applicants in accordance with Article 6 of the Passport Law.

3. Refrain from confiscating valid passports of Tibetans who return from foreign travel; also refrain from confiscating valid passports from Tibetans as a means of sanctioning religious, political or cultural expression that is viewed not to be compatible with the Party's official policies.

4. Allow Tibetans unhindered domestic travel and refrain from repressing expression of religious, political and cultural beliefs and activities.

5. Access to Tibet by foreigners, particularly if they happen to select Tibetan-run travel agencies, hotels and vendors, which will greatly help develop the local economy. Access to Tibet for Tibetan Americans particularly, would be a great fulfillment of the many personal aspirations to visit Tibet- whether to meet relatives or experience a pilgrimage to the homeland of their great teachers and ancestors.

Thank you.

2. Mr. Gershman, I'm sure you're aware of the overwhelming amount of vacancies at the State Department. One of those vacancies is the Special Coordinator for Tibetan Issues, established in the Tibetan Policy Act of 2002. How would you rate this Administration in carrying out the duties of the Tibetan Policy Act?

[NOTE: A response was not received by Mr. Carl Gershman prior to printing.]